I would like to dedicate this book to everyone who shares my passion for travel. I have run into many of you during my own travels, in airports, at hotels, taking in the sights, enjoying a meal...

Thank you to those of you who have taken the time to stop and talk to me; who have shared your stories, good and bad; and who have reminded me that there is something magical about a journey whether for relaxation or to learn something new.

To everyone who shares my view that a person's travels help to define who they are, I say a very heartfelt thank you.

Contents

Acknowledgements ix

Introduction xi

Chapter 1: Planning for Paradise

Initial Research: Setting the Stage 1
Group Vacations: When Three's Not a Crowd 6
Paperwork: Beyond the Red Tape 8
Customs and Taxes 13
Time-Zone Tango 14
Language: Breaking Down Barriers 14
Peak-Season Tips That Work All Year 16
Weathering the Weather 19
Perks and Upgrades: It's Always Worth Asking 20

Chapter 2: Insurance: Cover Yourself!

Protecting Your Travel Investment 23
Insurance: Your Safety Net 24
Cancellation and Interruption Insurance 26
Baggage and Personal Effects Insurance 27
Medical Insurance 28
Avoiding Disaster: Does a Travel Warning Void Your Travel Insurance? 30
Rescue Me: When You Need More Than Insurance 31
Cutting through the Red Tape: Making a Claim 31

Chapter 3: Ready... Set... Prepare!

A Little Preparation Goes a Long Way 35
Itineraries: Putting Time on Your Side 35
Currency: Show Me the Money! 36
Electrical Current: Don't Be Shocked! 40
Hands Off! Protecting Your Home While You're Away 41
Baggage: Don't Let It Weigh You Down 43
Making the Most of the Space You Have: The Art of Packing 45
Travel Funnies 50

Chapter 4: Staying Healthy

Healthy Travel Starts at Home 53
An Ounce of Prevention 54
Medication: A Movable Pharmacy 56
Lagging Behind: Jet Lag Solutions 56
Healthy Flight Plans 58
Deep Vein Thrombosis: DVT Danger 59
Water, Water, Everywhere... 59
Food for Thought 60
Motion Sickness: Oh, Those Waves 61
Oops! Common Maladies 61
"Medic!" Finding Medical Assistance 62
Insects and Other Critters 63
Handy Health Hints 63
Flying While Pregnant 64

Chapter 5: Staying Safe

"Is It Safe?" 69
The Official Word: Government Travel Advisories 69
Know Before You Go 70
Traveller Beware: Common Travel Traps 70
Safety First: En Route 74
Pickpocket Prevention 77
Help! What If I'm Robbed? 78
Girls Get Away Safely 78
Checking In: Staying Safe in a Hotel 79
Staying Safe When It's Not Safe 80
Prepare Like a Boy Scout: Pack These Essentials 80

Chapter 6: Air Travel: Flying High

Booking Your Flight 83
At the Airport 89
On the Flight 93
Playing the Luggage Lotto: Lost and Damaged Bags 96

Chapter 7: Cruises: A Life on the Waves

Oh, for the Ocean Blue 101
Information Central: Researching Your Cruise 103
Cruising with Children 104
Save Us a Cabin! Booking Your Cruise 106
A Berth with a View: Choosing Your Cabin 107
Getting to the Ship 107

Setting Sail: On-Board Advice 108
Land Ho: Disembarking 114

Chapter 8: On the Road: Renting a Vehicle

The Case for Rentals 117
Deals on Wheels: Making the Reservation 118
Fees, Fees, and More Fees 119
Vehicle Rental Insurance 121
Picking Up the Vehicle 122
Staying Safe on the Road 124
How to Handle Breakdowns and Damage 125
Returning the Vehicle 126
Roadworthy Notes 127

Chapter 9: Lodgings: Where to Lay Your Head

What's Your Style? 129
Swap Meet! Exchanging Your Home 131
Hot Tips for Hotels 132

Chapter 10: Logistical Logic: On the Trip

Put On a Happy Face 143
The Art of Tipping 144
Cultural Sensitivities 146
Calling Home 148
Shop 'Til You Drop... or Not 150
We're Leaving When? Schedule Changes 153
Oh No! Lost Passports 153

Chapter 11: All in the Family: Travelling with Kids

Keeping It in the Family 157
Before You Leave Home 160
Teenage Trials and Tribulations 161
Sky High: Flying with Children 162
Travelling with Babies and Toddlers 164
Surviving a Car Trip 165
Going It Alone: Single-Parent Travel 165
Flying Solo: Children Travelling Alone 166

Chapter 12: Specialty Travel

Theme Park Thrills 169
When the Honeymoon's Just Beginning 170
Travel in Good Company: Guided Tours 172
Lifelong Learning 173

Adventure Travel 174
Volunteer Vacations 174
Girls' Getaways and "Man-cations" 175
Accessible Travel 175
Bringing Along Your Best Buddy: Travelling with Pets 176
Business Travel 177

Chapter 13: Coming Home

Duty-Free Bargains... or Not 181
A Taxing Reminder 181
The Last Red Tape: Going through Immigration and Customs 181
Readjusting to Life at Home 182

Checklists

To-do List 184
Packing Lists 186

Useful Travel Websites 188

Index 191

Acknowledgements

Writing my first book was a daunting task, and one that I could never have completed without the love and support of many people.

To everyone at Global TV, thank you for being so supportive of this book.

Thanks to the best team in the travel business... the staff at Jubilee Travel. To the management team—Wendy Lanphear, Shauna Zeck, Carmen Howe, and Ellie Brown—thank you for allowing me the freedom to write in the full and comforting knowledge that everything else was being taken care of.

To my best friend, Lisa Dalton, who encouraged me every step of the way. Thank you for reading my manuscript over and over again.

To my twin brother, John Newell, and my wee brother, Steven Newell, thank you for always being there when I need you.

To my parents, John and Sylvia Newell, who put a poster on my bedroom wall when I was eight years old that read: "Whatever the challenge, whatever the test, whatever you're striving for, give it your best." Thank you for always believing in me.

Finally, thank you to my amazing husband, Jeff, and my two beautiful children, Lauren and Grant, for always loving and supporting me. I am such a lucky woman!

Introduction

I love travel. That may not come as a surprise once you know that, for the past 14 years, I've run my own travel agency. I also talk regularly about travel on TV and radio, and write about travel for newspapers and magazines. But for me, travel is so much more than what I do. It's who I really am. It's my passion. My best childhood memories are of travelling with my parents and my two brothers. Now that I have a family of my own, travelling has become a way to create similar wonderful memories for a new generation. It also reinforces my connections with other family members as we often choose to travel together as a way to spend time with each other.

When I travel, no matter where I go, it's a chance to enjoy some downtime without computers or cellphones. It's an opportunity for rest and rejuvenation. I return feeling energized by my journey, and by the new people and places that I've encountered.

Every trip creates its own memories as well as its own moments, moments that stay with you forever. Like photographs, you can take them out whenever you want to, surrounding yourself with the sights and scents and sounds of a place that for some reason, at that exact moment, was something special for you. Maybe it's the view of mountain peaks rising far above you, seeming to pierce the sky; or the sound of a child's laughter as they play on a white sand beach; or the glow of a candle as dusk falls over an intimate dinner. These are the memories that help you through long, dark winters.

Your moments will be unique to you and your travels. They may be fleeting, but they will always be yours. This is what travel does. It takes us out of our ordinary lives, and shows us that we share a truly remarkable world with each other. In many ways, I believe that travel makes us more complete as human beings.

As you read the pages that follow, planning and enjoying your own travels, I wish you many magical moments and marvellous memories.

Claire Newell

Chapter 1

Planning for Paradise

Initial Research: Setting the Stage

Planning a trip is half the fun of travelling. In fact, I can think of few things that are better than having a trip to look forward to. And yet, over the years, I've seen far too many people book a trip without researching it properly before they go. Those are also the people who often have unrealistic expectations of their trip, which can lead to unhappy travellers.

You can't imagine how much more you'll enjoy your trip if you do your research, and not just before you choose your destination, but after you make your choice, too. You'll find must-see sights, off-the-beaten-path cafés, and all kinds of tips to make the trip easier and much more fun. Reading brochures, surfing the Internet, and talking to people who have actually been to the destination are all so important when making your decisions. All this research can also be a wonderful way to get started on a travel diary or scrapbook—which are two ways to keep the magic of travel alive in your thoughts, even after the trip is finished!

It's vital that you look into anything and everything that may affect your vacation: cultural differences, language, weather, documentation requirements, currency, politics. Everything. With the easy access that we have to all kinds of information these days, it's right there at your fingertips. Ultimately you choose how you travel, so do your homework! And do it early—the sooner you start making travel plans, the better chance you'll have of being able to travel when and where you want to.

ASKING THE BIG QUESTIONS

Speaking of planning, how exactly do you decide where to go? First, prioritize your wish list for the vacation. Are you looking for relaxation or adventure, culture or entertainment, the beach or local festivals, family time or couple time?

Being aware of your goals—and being realistic about who you are and what you like—always makes it easier to determine whether the destinations you're considering will fulfill your vacation needs and desires.

Second, you'll make some of your decisions based on how long you can be away, whether it's a weekend getaway or a half-year, round-the-world cruise.

Third, although it's tempting to try to see as many things as possible during a visit, avoid overscheduling yourself. You may enjoy yourself more if you're not racing from one place to the next the whole time. In fact, it's often worth building in an "easy" first day, especially if you know you'll be very busy in the days leading up to your departure, or if the journey will take you across several time zones.

Fourth, think about how you want to travel. If you've never been to Italy, you may opt for a tour that takes in the whole country to let you see a smattering of everything the country has to offer. It may turn out to be a "taster" trip for a future vacation. Many travellers today, however, are choosing to narrow their focus, staying instead in one or two areas and getting to know them in greater depth. This allows you to spend more time enjoying your vacation, rather than simply going from place to place, but it's up to you. There's nothing wrong with wanting to cover a lot of ground, as long as that's your choice and your budget can cope.

LOOKING FOR ANSWERS

It's probably easier to figure out where not to look when it comes to researching your trip, as you can easily find yourself overwhelmed by information overload. Internet websites and traditional brochures and guidebooks make excellent starting points when you're making destination decisions. (If you decide to take a guidebook with you, it's a good idea to tear out just the pages you'll need, to avoid using up your precious baggage allowance.)

> www Expanding your research beyond the regular sources can really add depth and value to your travels, however. Try looking for novels, non-fiction books, movies, television shows, and magazines that deal with travel, historical, or cultural subjects to illuminate and enlighten your days on the road. You can also check for special events at local libraries or art galleries. To give you the sense of an area before you travel, I recommend watching travel videos on the Internet. My favourite sites are www.flyingmonk.com and www.turnhere.com.

TRAVEL AGENTS: A TRAVELLER'S BEST FRIEND

In this Internet age, it's tempting to do it all yourself. However, don't rule out travel agents just yet. Remember that they spend their days researching the best ways to reach destinations around the world, and the best ways to enjoy them once you're there. They can do more than just book a vacation for you; they're travel professionals, so they can provide many services that you just can't find elsewhere. Think of them as your expert travel counsellor.

Because they have relationships with travel providers, travel agents can also wield considerable buying power, which in turn can give you deals that are better than anything you can expect to find if you're booking your own travel. Agents also often have access to special discounts or upgrades that aren't available on the Internet or through tour operators directly.

The training and knowledge that travel agents have may save you time as well as money, especially if they can provide one-stop shopping for all your travel needs. And since they're often travellers themselves, their firsthand experience can offer you ideas that you might not have thought of, tips for travelling success, and surefire advice for great trips. Agents can also provide essential advice about travel regulations, paperwork requirements, and insurance options, so don't hesitate to ask any questions that you may have.

In many travel agencies, all these services come free of charge to you, the consumer. Some travel agencies do charge booking or research fees, however, so it's always good to check on those before you start working with an agent. But even in cases where fees apply, knowing that the advice of a professional is only a phone call or e-mail away can prove to be a sound investment. That's because a good travel agent can become invaluable when problems arise, whether it's re-booking flights interrupted by a natural disaster, or transferring hotels if there's a major cleanliness issue.

 Travel Best Bet!
Immediately after Hurricane Wilma hit the Cancún area of Mexico, travel agencies worked overtime to get their clients out of the affected areas on the best possible flights, or arranged ground travel to move them to unaffected areas of Mexico so that they could finish their vacations. When you book through a trusted travel agent, you're not alone, even in a worst-case scenario.

Of course, you do need to choose your travel agent carefully. Ideally, you should look for a good agent who works for a good agency. Following up on recommendations from friends and relatives who use an agent they trust is an excellent plan. In most cases, an agency that handles general travel will be able to handle a good range of different vacations and destinations, particularly as many of its agents should be trained in various specialties, such as cruise vacations. However, it's worth looking for a specialist agency, or at least an agent trained in a particular specialty, if you're doing something that could use a more detailed depth of knowledge (adventure travel, cruising, and volunteer tourism come to mind).

When you're looking for an agency, you should always ask how long they've been in business, what kind of ongoing training their agents receive, and whether the agency belongs to industry associations such as the Association of Canadian Travel Agents, the Better Business Bureau, and the Cruise Line Industry Association.

The best way to check their track record is through your local Better Business Bureau. They'll probably have a phone number or URL that you can use to find out whether the agency has had complaints about its services, and whether those complaints were resolved to the satisfaction of the customer.

Warning signs or red flags that you're dealing with an unethical or unreliable agent would include, for example, being asked for extra fees in order to secure special cabins or hotel rooms, over and above the actual cost of those cabins or rooms. It's also important for agents to return calls promptly and provide itineraries or documents when they say they will, and to be knowledgeable about your destination or vacation choice and honest with you if they don't have that knowledge at their fingertips.

It's important to work with an agent who takes the time to understand what you're looking for from a vacation. Agents should be able to guide you to places that suit your needs, they should be happy to answer your questions, and they should always be organized (including getting back to you with results or progress reports in a timely way). Don't hesitate to shop around a little to find a travel professional who's a good "fit" for you and your family.

Travel agencies do sometimes go out of business, unfortunately. If this happens to you while you're working with an agency, the first thing you need to establish is whether or not the defunct travel agency has paid the travel supplier (the airline, hotel, tour operator, etc.) for your trip. If they have, then you have nothing to worry about and you can go on your trip as planned.

If they haven't paid the travel supplier, then the first line of defence is compensation through the credit card company that you used to purchase the trip. That's why I **ALWAYS** recommend paying by credit card versus cash or cheque. You can also try for compensation through your travel insurance provider.

Consumers who book with an agency registered in British Columbia, Ontario, or Quebec have some added protection. In these provinces, there is a fund (the BC Travel Assurance Fund in British Columbia, the Travel Compensation Fund in Ontario, and the Fonds d'indemnisation des clients des agents de voyages in Quebec) that provides a possible source of compensation when consumers do not receive the travel services they purchased and are unable to obtain compensation through their travel insurance, credit card, or other sources. Check with your local provincial government's information line or Internet site for the latest contact information for these funds.

TRAVEL ADVISORIES AND WARNINGS: PAY ATTENTION!

If you have any concerns about health, political unrest, or personal safety in a destination, the US, British, and Canadian governments all issue regular advisories and warnings to their citizens, noting trouble spots and precautions. You can find them at:

- Canada: www.voyage.gc.ca
- United Kingdom: www.fco.gov.uk
- United States: http://travel.state.gov

You can read about government travel advisories in more detail in Chapter 5, Staying Safe.

THE INTERNET: WHY IT TRULY IS THE WORLD WIDE WEB

The Internet is a fantastic research tool for travellers. You can "chat" with fellow travellers to learn about their experiences, share great tips for dining and accommodation, preview a wide range of travel options, and generally get a feel for your destination before you arrive. It's no wonder that it's increasingly becoming the tool of choice for researching travel.

It's not without its drawbacks, however. One British couple was researching flights to Sydney, Australia, and found a great price on the Internet. The only trouble was that they actually ended up in Sydney, Nova Scotia, Canada. They were met with a warm welcome, but obviously it wasn't their first choice.

So yes, it's buyer beware on the World Wide Web. If you do decide to use it to book your vacation, be sure to think through all the details beyond just the price and use your common sense. Check out the Useful Travel Websites listing at the back of this book to get started.

Travel Best Bet!
A friend booked tickets online for herself, her daughter, and her daughter's two small children to take a charter flight from Canada to London, England, and then another flight on to Provence, in France. Unfortunately, she didn't realize that the charter flight arrived at Gatwick Airport, while the flight to France left from Heathrow

> *Airport. Both airports are technically considered Lon-*
> *don, but they're miles apart from each other. She didn't*
> *leave enough connection time between the two flights,*
> *and didn't realize that the family's luggage couldn't be*
> *checked directly through to France. The error was costly*
> *from several perspectives: a missed connection, time with*
> *toddlers at an airport, the expense of purchasing a new*
> *set of tickets, and, from a personal perspective, an extra*
> *dose of stress.*

If you're booking online, just be sure that you're aware of any logistical issues that may be involved. Do your research thoroughly, and double-check everything before you press the "book" key on your computer screen, including the following:

- Dates
- Destinations
- Departure and arrival times of flights and other transportation
- Arrival and departure terminals at airports
- Transit time required between terminals at airports
- Transit time required between airports and other destinations
- Final costs (including taxes and fees)
- Refund or change requirements and fees
- Visa and passport requirements

Group Vacations: When Three's Not a Crowd

It's easier to get a group together than many people think and, because groups qualify for special rates, it can be worth your while to consider this option. Before you throw up your hands in horror at the prospect of setting off with several dozen people in tow, you should know that, depending on the travel, groups can be as few as 10 people. That's just two families, or perhaps a bridal party, or even a sports team. But whether you're travelling with ten people or a thousand people, here's some advice to keep the planning manageable.

Choose one key person to head up the group. This person should be organized, efficient, and a good decision-maker. (Some diplomatic skill is a bonus.) They should be equipped with all the contact information for anyone interested in being part of the group and should be able to coordinate the distribution of information. E-mail can be an excellent way to coordinate planning, but be aware that it can become cumbersome if everyone in the group responds to every message. It's also important for the organizer to activate the "read receipt" option for e-mails about the trip so that they know that everyone has received and read the e-mail. This avoids a situation where someone claims not to know a key piece of information because they didn't receive it. You may consider using a private group e-mail forum for posting updates if everyone in your group is comfortable with this approach. Yahoo! Groups (http://groups.yahoo.com) is one option: it's free, and you can restrict the group to only your members.

The key person should have the authority to limit the number of choices offered to the group. That's because the more choices you give a group of people, the longer it takes for them to decide on just one option. Accept the fact that no single spot will please everyone—just aim to satisfy the majority.

Be patient with your travel adviser or agent. You should expect to receive group quotes at least 48 to 72 hours after the initial requests. It's reasonable to follow up with the agent if you haven't heard anything for 72 hours, unless of course the agent warned you that it would take longer. Most companies need to ensure that there is enough space, have the price approved by a senior employee, and then prepare the document to be sent back to you. Group rates tend to be significantly better than individual rates, though, so it's usually worth the wait.

Get firm commitments. Once a trip has been agreed upon, the key person should make sure that everyone who has expressed an interest really intends to go. There is no better way to do that than by asking people to put their money where their mouth is. I recommend taking deposits and payments as early as possible, and definitely as soon as the trip has been confirmed, to ensure that no payment deadlines are missed. Otherwise you risk automatic cancellation of any part of the trip or leaving one person (most probably you, if you're the key person) holding the bag!

If you're using a travel agent to book a group trip, I usually suggest that the key person be the only one initially in contact with the agent. Until plans have been confirmed, too many people contacting the travel agent just creates mass confusion. It can be handy to sit down with the group during the planning stage to compile a list of questions for the agent. That way, the key person will remember to ask all the questions and can then keep a note of the answers. Once the plans are finalized and it's time for payment, the key person should instruct each group member to contact the travel agent directly to go over any questions they may have, to discuss travel insurance, and to apply payment. Group insurance is something you should discuss at length with your agent, because it's not always the best option, especially for groups of fewer than 16 people.

When planning, consider building "flexible" time into the itinerary to accommodate the different interests of people within the group. Days, or even portions of days, that aren't scheduled allow people to team up to explore an area on their own, enjoy a round of golf, relax in a local spa, or even head out for a solo couple of hours.

Paperwork: Beyond the Red Tape

Since the September 11, 2001, terrorist attacks on the United States, security has become a major issue worldwide, with the result that proper personal identification is essential when travelling. Prior to 2001, crossing the border between some countries required little more than one piece of government-issued identification. It didn't even need to have a picture on it. And it used to be that when you booked an airline ticket, you could use only your first initial and last name. These days, if you're just one letter "off" you will likely be denied boarding the aircraft. In fact, you now need to ensure that at least one piece of valid identification matches the name on the ticket exactly, so it's important to pay attention to these details.

In addition, the US is bringing in stricter border-crossing requirements for identification documents. Although it's likely that they'll eventually accept some form of special travel identification for Canadian travellers, they're currently requiring passports for all air travellers, to be extended to travellers arriving by land and sea by January 1, 2008.

Travel Best Bet!
One of our clients who recently booked an airline ticket with us gave her middle name, which she goes by, instead of her legal first name. She was denied boarding by the airline because her identification showed her first name and so didn't match the name on her ticket. Luckily she was able to find a notary public at the airport (they're not always on duty) and obtain a notarized letter that enabled her to travel. The process was time-consuming, however, and expensive.

No matter where you're travelling to, take the time to find out exactly what documentation you'll need for entry. And give yourself plenty of time to get it in order. Remember that obtaining the appropriate documentation for your trip is your responsibility. Even the best cancellation insurance in the world won't cover your oversight on this one. And not only do you need to check the documentation that's needed for entry into the country you're travelling to, but you also need to check the documentation needed for you to get back into the country you're travelling from, and any countries that you may be travelling to during your trip. You can get the information for entry and exit requirements for most countries online at www.voyage.gc.ca. Just click on the Travel Reports & Warnings option.

Personally, I wouldn't travel anywhere these days without a passport. My advice is to apply for a passport, and then use it. It's the safest and most efficient document for travel in today's world.

PASSPORTS: YOUR TICKET TO THE WORLD

A valid passport, good for at least six months beyond the intended length of stay in your destination, is strongly recommended, if not essential, for travelling to many countries. Each individual—even a newborn baby—must now carry his or her own passport. When you apply for your passport (the application forms can be obtained from various government offices and agencies), read all the instructions carefully, including those that apply to photographs, to children under the age of 16, and to guarantors (those who sign your passport application). You can expect to present a birth certificate (photocopies are not permitted), citizenship papers or citizenship card (if applicable), specially sized photographs (available at almost any camera store or photographer's studio), and the signatures of two guarantors.

You should note that the introduction of new facial recognition technology means strict guidelines for passport photographs, including the need for black and white photos and non-smiling expressions with no teeth showing. You can also expect immigration officials to ask you to remove your hat or headscarf if you're wearing one at the airport so that they can better check your appearance against your passport photograph.

Passports in many countries are now taking longer to process than they did previously, so ensure that you apply for yours well in advance of your travel. For the quickest service, visit a passport office in person if possible, especially if you need a rush passport. You can often designate in writing another person to pick up the completed passport for you if necessary, but of course it needs to be you who applies for it. No one can do that part for you. Otherwise, follow the instructions for mailing your application, and be sure to register or otherwise protect your paperwork while it's in the mail.

These websites can help you with the application forms and rules:

- Canada: www.voyage.gc.ca
- United Kingdom: www.ukps.gov.uk
- United States: http://travel.state.gov

When I was in the airport recently, I noticed a problem at the ticket counter next to me. A couple that was on their way to Switzerland was being denied boarding. The problem was that their passports, which they'd been issued at the same time some years before, were expiring in two months. Entry rules for Switzerland require a passport that is good for at least 90 days. Switzerland isn't the only country with this type of rule. The length of time varies, and can be as long as six months (as it is for Israel, for example), so it's vital that you check the country's requirements and make sure your passport meets them. Start your research at www.voyage.gc.ca.

If you travel a great deal you should also check how many passport pages you have left, because—like the passport expiration rule—you may need a certain number of blank pages left in your passport to be allowed entry into certain countries. Other requirements when you're entering a country that's not your own may include visas, proof that you can support yourself while you're in the country without working there, and an airline ticket for the next leg of your journey. Some countries also routinely ask you for a destination address while you're in their country, so it's good to have the name and address of your hotel handy.

DUAL CITIZENSHIP DILEMMAS

If you're a citizen of more than one country, the laws of both of those countries may still apply to you, even if you're not a resident there. This may be further complicated if one or more of the countries doesn't recognize your other citizenship. In some cases, travellers who are visiting a country to which they hold (or once held) citizenship can trigger issues such as any compulsory military service required by that country. Always check with all the appropriate governments to ensure that you don't encounter any unpleasant surprises. People have been caught in the past when their journey was re-routed to an unexpected stopover point because of weather or other urgent situations.

Some people like to travel with more than one passport, usually to speed through customs and immigration line-ups at certain airports by using the passport of the country they're entering. I don't recommend this because it can prompt questions from immigration officials about why you're using different passports. It's possible that they'll consider it a red flag. However, if you do choose to carry two passports, ensure that they contain exactly the same personal information about you, right down to the spelling of your name.

In addition, only use one of the passports when crossing into a different country. The two passports should never be kept together, nor should they be shown together. Keep one with you at all times and keep the other in your carry-on luggage. As well, when you reach your destination, I recommend you keep one in the hotel safe and the other on your person.

WHO'S GOING WHERE: VISAS AND TOURIST CARDS

Visas, which are essentially a country's approval for you to enter for a particular purpose and length of time, are required for many destinations. You'll more than likely be advised by your travel agent or airline if this is necessary, but ultimately it's your responsibility to find out if you need one. I recommend going to www.visaconnection.com for the most current information about visa requirements. Your travel agent may be able to help you with the process of obtaining the necessary visas, but normally you apply directly to the country you plan to visit through their nearest embassy or consulate. In some cases you'll obtain the visa at the airport on arrival. It's essential to know ahead of time which countries require visas and how to apply for them.

If you're only making a flight connection within a country, you likely won't need a visa. For most countries, Canadians are not required to obtain a visa if you're transiting within 24 hours and staying within the transit area (i.e., the international airport). However, you should always check each country in which you're landing.

Tourist or landing cards are documents that governments use to keep track of people crossing both into and out of their country, and are applicable in some countries (e.g., tourist cards in Cuba, the Dominican Republic, and Mexico, and landing cards in the UK). These cards will be available at the airport once you arrive or will be handed out on the aircraft before you land at your destination. Be careful when filling them out because you may have to pay for a new one (anywhere from US$10 to several hundred dollars depending on the country) and potentially go through a whole lot of hassle (such as standing in a line-up for several hours) to get it. Some countries do not allow any strikethroughs or scribbles on the cards, so take your time completing them. In some countries you may be given a card on arrival that you need to keep until you leave. Keep the card safe with your passport, so that you don't lose it.

TAKING THE KIDS? TAKE THE RIGHT PAPERS!

If you're travelling with children you need to be especially careful to have the correct paperwork with you, particularly if the children aren't your own, don't have the same last name as you do, or you're travelling without your partner. A notarized consent form signed by the other parent, or by both parents depending on the situation, is the standard that many countries require. In Canada, lawyers and notary publics use a standardized form letter on which they simply fill in the appropriate names, dates, and destinations. It takes minutes to process the letter, which will typically cost between C$25 and C$50. It's also a good idea to get a new consent form for each trip, just to be safe. Without the right paperwork, you could be refused boarding by the airline, or you could be denied entry by local immigration officials. (See Chapter 11, All in the Family: Travelling with Kids, for more on this.)

 Travel Best Bet!
One family I know booked a vacation and took along a friend of one of their children. Unfortunately, they didn't have the proper documentation (that is, a notarized letter from the child's parents stating that they had permission to take the child on vacation with them) to take the friend out of Canada. Luckily, there was a notary public on duty at the airport, so they were able to get the letter in time to board the flight— although at a hefty price! It also involved the child's parents having to come down to the airport to sign the letter, plus several trips back and forth through security, so the hassle factor was considerable.

ON THE ROAD, WITH INTERNATIONAL DRIVING PERMITS

If you plan on renting a vehicle in another country, you should know that the United Nations established the international driving permit back in 1949 to make it easier for qualified motorists to drive in foreign countries. Language barriers can obviously create difficulties for both motorists and police so the document is printed in eight languages: the six official languages of the United Nations (Arabic, Chinese, English, French, Russian, and Spanish) and German and Japanese. Although you likely won't need an international driving permit— just your regular licence is usually sufficient—if you're American or Canadian and you're renting a car outside North America, the international driving permit is recommended by most countries, and required by some, for driving and for vehicle or motorcycle rental, whether you're travelling for business or pleasure.

The identification is easy to apply for (automobile association offices in your country of residence can often provide them) and you don't have to take any kind of test. You'll need to have your government-issued driver's licence with you when you apply, and you must apply before you leave for your trip. You probably won't need a special appointment for this. Just show up at the office with your licence, and the permit will be issued while you wait. When you drive in the foreign country, you must have both your regular driver's licence and the inter-national driving permit (which will list any of your original licence's conditions, such as the requirement to wear corrective lenses for vision) with you. Keep in mind that an international driving permit simply allows you to drive in a foreign country, it is **NOT** insurance. Be sure to obtain insurance separately. (See

Chapter 8, On the Road: Renting a Vehicle, for more details on driving and insurance.)

Customs and Taxes

Whether you're crossing international borders by planes, trains, or automobiles, customs regulations will be an issue. When you travel by rail or by road you'll normally find the customs office at the physical border location. When you're flying, you'll either clear customs for your destination before you board your plane, between one connecting flight and the next, or at your final destination. But be aware that customs closes at different times in different airports. Check with the airport website for these times.

Travel Best Bet!
One couple who needed to clear customs before leaving Canada for the United States discovered on arriving at the airport that their flight had been delayed until 11 p.m. They decided to go for dinner before going through security and customs, blissfully unaware that customs closed at 8 p.m. Since they arrived at customs after the office had closed, they weren't able to clear customs and were therefore denied boarding and forced to pay for a flight the next day!

The process of clearing customs will vary depending on the country involved, but every country imposes limits on what visitors and its own nationals can bring in. Check with your government and the countries you're visiting to make sure that you know what the duty- or tax-free limits are (it may be a sliding scale that lets you bring in greater quantities for longer trips). Whatever you do, don't assume that because your vacation destination bills itself as "duty" or "tax" free, you can bring in as much of its goods as you want. It's duty or tax free there—not at home.

These websites list duty-free allowances that may apply to you:

- Canada: www.cbsa-asfc.gc.ca
- United Kingdom: www.hmrc.gov.uk
- United States: www.cbp.gov

Be sure to keep your receipts, both for items such as accommodation (which will help prove how long you've been out of the country) and for the items that you've bought. If you're taking a relatively new piece of electronic equipment or jewellery with you, customs officers may assume that you purchased it while you were away, rather than before you left. To prove that you bought it at home, carry a photocopy of the receipt for it (showing the serial number), or register it before you leave the country at your local customs office. This will ensure that it's not subject to any confusion—or duties—when you bring it back home. (For more on customs and duty free, see Chapter 13, Coming Home.)

Time-Zone Tango

The world has 25 time zones, which can sometimes be difficult to keep track of when you're travelling through them. They're all measured east and west from the "prime meridian," which is located at Greenwich, England. In addition, some countries have adopted non-standard time zones, usually offset by 30 minutes (e.g., Newfoundland in Canada). Civilian time-zone designations (there are military designations as well) use three-letter abbreviations: GMT for Greenwich Mean Time, for example, and EST for Eastern Standard Time.

When you're researching your destination, checking its time zone will help to guide your trip planning. I recommend www.timeanddate.com for the local time and date in hundreds of cities around the world, which is excellent for keeping track of exactly what day it is in Asia and Australia. You'll also find www.worldtimezone.com useful for showing time zones around the world, and for figuring out the time difference between different places. Keep in mind that not all countries—or even regions within a country—observe daylight savings time, and they don't always change back and forth on the same day. This can be especially important given that your tickets will show local times.

Travel Best Bet!
A friend of mine was travelling from Maine to Nova Scotia by car en route to the ferry that runs between St. John, New Brunswick, and Digby, Nova Scotia. She'd carefully figured out how long the trip would take, but didn't realize until she crossed the US-Canadian border that the clocks went ahead by an hour in New Brunswick. That lost hour was enough to make her miss the ferry sailing. Oops!

Language: Breaking Down Barriers

If you're travelling to a country that doesn't share your mother tongue as its official language, don't automatically think of the language differences as a barrier to communicating with the people at your destination. Instead, try to find ways to make that barrier disappear. The effort you put into preparing yourself for the language issues you may face will definitely be worth it!

IS ENGLISH THE UNIVERSAL LANGUAGE?

In the world of tourism, it seems that English really is the universal language. It's the standard for air traffic control, and you'll find English spoken to some degree at most airports, in better hotels, and on board cruise ships. In many countries, signs will appear in the official language and also in English, and in some cases, in additional languages such as French, Spanish, German, Mandarin, or Japanese, depending on where most of their tourists come from. For example, many retail stores in the Canadian mountain community of Banff, Alberta, post signs in Japanese, because they receive a significant number of visitors from Japan. Always remember, though, that wherever you are, you're a guest. While it's wonderful if your destination caters to English-speaking travellers, you shouldn't expect it of them. Instead, use the approach that it's your responsibility as a traveller to prepare yourself for language issues.

For example, front-line staff at many international resorts will most probably speak a variety of languages, including English. Support staff such as cleaners, however, may have only a few words of English, so adjust your expectations accordingly.

I JUST DON'T UNDERSTAND! STRATEGIES FOR COMMUNICATING

When you travel, it's truly amazing what a small attempt to use some key phrases in the local language will accomplish. "Please," "Thank you," "You're welcome," "Good morning/afternoon/evening," "How much is this?" and "Where are the washrooms?" will go a long way towards getting better service from non-English speakers. (Simple phrase books are a great asset in such situations.) It's also a wonderful recognition of the local culture. Your efforts to learn those phrases will very often be met with smiles and warm welcomes. Learning important phrases in different languages can be done in all sorts of ways. You could take language classes, buy audio lessons on CD, or pick up a language book from a library or bookstore.

Another option may be to invest in a computerized pocket translator. These devices allow you to enter a common phrase in one language, which it will then translate into the language you need. Pocket translators have become increasingly affordable and compact over the years. They're a good investment if you plan on travelling regularly into areas where you don't know the language.

Be prepared for potential difficulties, though. For example, if you're using a taxi, write down the address and phone number of your hotel in the local language, as well as your destination's address and phone number, and carry them with you. Many hotels make this easy for you by offering small business cards that you can tuck into your pocket. The concierge can help you with the local spelling for your destination, if necessary.

Phrase books can really help you out with the language, and they're certainly a sign that you're making an effort, which is always appreciated. Just be aware that if you ask a question in a foreign language, you're likely to be answered in that language. If you can't understand the answer, you can ask the speaker to repeat it more slowly, or you could ask if they speak English. You can also point to the question on the page if you're struggling with the pronunciation. Just remember that if you're in a country that uses the Cyrillic alphabet, for example, and you're using a phrase book with Roman letters (which make the pronunciation easier for English speakers) the native speaker may not be able to read the transliteration in your book. Still, even with these caveats, phrase books are definitely worth carrying.

Peak-Season Tips That Work All Year

If you're travelling during a destination's peak (or busiest) season, there are plenty of things that you can do to make your travels as stress-free as possible. These tips work well at any time of the year, but they're invaluable at peak times. And always remember the traveller's motto: Flexible, Organized, and Prepared!

WHAT TO KNOW BEFORE YOU GO

The best thing that you can do for yourself to make peak-season travel easier is to book every portion of your travel, from flights to hotel rooms, and car rental to attraction admission, as far in advance as possible.

Your willingness to be flexible with your schedule can make a big difference when you're booking, both for availability and for cost. Choosing to fly on off-peak dates, even within a busy holiday season, will help you to miss the heaviest crowds. (For example, flying on December 25 may actually be easier than the days leading up to it, because people often prefer not to travel on the holiday itself.) Always aim for non-stop flights to make it less likely that you—or your bags—will miss a connection. And if you fly on the first flight of the day you'll be the first in line for alternative seats for the rest of the day if your flight ends up being cancelled.

Try to purchase attraction or museum tickets in advance if possible. If you want to visit a particularly popular attraction at your destination (such as the Louvre Museum in Paris), find out if it offers an advance ticketing option. Reserving your ticket for a specific date and time (often from the comfort of your travel agent's office or on your home computer) will let you avoid many of the line-ups. In some cases (such as the Uffizi Gallery and other popular museums in Florence, Italy), you won't be charged for the ticket until you show up, which means that if you don't make it to the attraction for some reason, you won't lose your money. Be sure to take your reservation documentation with you as proof of purchase.

Find out if your airline offers an online check-in option where you can check in for your flight and print out your boarding pass from your personal computer. This saves you time at the airport, because you'll be able to check your bags in through an express baggage line.

Even if your ticket information says that you don't need to reconfirm your flights, I still recommend double-checking your flight schedule and seat assignment with the airline a day ahead of your flight. Also check the weather forecast and the local news. If weather delays look likely, call the airline or check their website for potential changes to your flight schedule. Flights can be delayed for a number of reasons such as weather, mechanical problems, or unexpected passenger situations. That's why checking your flight on the airline's website just before you leave for the airport, and being prepared for delays announced at the airport, is also a good idea. It's also worth checking the departures page on the airport's website.

When it comes to packing, keep your luggage as light as possible. If you're stuck at an airport, the lighter your luggage, the happier you'll be. For holiday travel, more and more people are now shipping packages or gifts instead of taking them on board the aircraft. This makes their luggage lighter, and eliminates the problems of cramped carry-on space on board the aircraft and potential damage to the contents of checked luggage. If you do choose to carry gifts with you, security regulations require them to be unwrapped to allow officials to inspect them. (For more on luggage and packing, see "Baggage" and "Making the Most of the Space You Have" in Chapter 3, Ready... Set... Prepare!)

EN-ROUTE ADVICE 1 → 2 → 3

At any time of the year, but especially during peak travel periods, give yourself plenty of time at the airport for check-in, security clearance, and arrival at your gate. This also means building in extra time to get to the airport. Find out what your airport is like during busy periods. Do roads and parking lots become congested? If they do, opt for a taxi, airport shuttle, or even a friend, rather than adding your own vehicle to the mix (and increasing your stress level). If you do drive yourself and park, make a note of where you've left your vehicle and put your vehicle claim ticket in a safe place in your wallet. You'll be amazed at how difficult it is to remember whether you're in the Park & Jet lot or the Park 'n' Fly lot after a few days away!

You'll probably have plenty of time in line to get your tickets and photo identification out for inspection by airline officials and to check that your luggage is properly tagged. Keep your luggage close (and preferably physically attached) to you at all times: airports are prime targets for theft, especially when they're crowded with people who have travel, not luggage, on their minds.

Don't push it when it comes to luggage allowances. More stringent security regulations, and packed planes, mean that flight crews will likely be enforcing the carry-on bag limits per person.

Finally, you should be aware that overbooked flights aren't unusual during busy periods. If you can be flexible about delaying your travel by a few hours, you may be able to earn extra frequent flyer miles, tickets, or upgrades. The airline will announce this prior to boarding.

HAPPY LANDINGS

Every once in a while, someone walks away from a baggage carousel—intentionally or otherwise—with a bag that doesn't belong to them. To avoid being a victim, don't delay getting to the baggage carousel to pick up your bags, and always double-check that the bag you've picked up from the carousel is really your own. To make your bags easier to identify, I recommend tying something bright and bold on the outside of your luggage that clearly makes it unique. It will also help to prevent someone from taking your bags by accident.

Expect long line-ups for airport shuttles and taxis when it's busy. You can try booking ahead to make sure that a driver will be there to pick you up, or ask a friend to pick you up (call them, preferably using a cellphone, when you have your luggage, and meet them at the pick-up area outside the arrivals part of the terminal).

ON THE GROUND

A good tip for beating the crowds while you're at your vacation destination is to check out opening times for the attractions you'll be visiting. That way you can plan to arrive as early as possible in the morning, before the crowds build. Alternatively, plan to visit in the evening when other people are more likely to be having dinner. Just double-check that the attraction is open late, of course.

Also look for alternatives to the busiest spots. Whether you're seeking beaches, restaurants, or golf, you may find that your hotel or travel agent can recommend places that are off the beaten track, but still close enough to be accessible. Make reservations wherever possible to avoid wasting time in line-ups and to ensure that you can actually get into the place that you're counting on seeing. It's true that once you've arrived at your destination you may be able to find cut-price tickets for activities such as theatre performances. Waiting to book this way is a trade-off, however, between the potential for saving money and the time spent in line that you could have spent doing something more enjoyable. It's all a matter of priorities. Spend your time on the things that mean more to you and you'll get the best out of your vacation.

These tips should help avert many potential vacation-travel headaches. Some hassles are unavoidable and utterly beyond your control, however. In those circumstances, the best you can do is to just take a deep breath, try to relax, and enjoy knowing that you had the foresight to bring along plenty of games, DVDs, or reading material.

Weathering the Weather

I know from experience that the weather can make or break your trip. Although there's never a guarantee, you can improve your odds by researching the typical weather at your destination during the dates you want to travel.

Many airlines, hotels, and tour companies will use reduced rates to entice you to travel to destinations during the "shoulder" or "low" season, when demand is lower—often because the weather is less than ideal. You have to decide what's more important to you: more chance of good weather and enjoying a destination to its full potential, or saving some money and seeing a destination regardless of what the weather may be.

 I like www.theweathernetwork.com or www.weather.com for checking weather around the world. Remember, too, that if a weather disaster affects your trip, you should contact your travel agent or your trip cancellation/interruption insurance company for assistance as soon as possible.

WINTERY TRAVEL: BRRR!

Snow, cold, fog, freezing rain, wind. Winter's tough on travellers! Add busy airports and missed connections, and you get the picture—it's not pretty. Be prepared for delays, from flight cancellations to waits for aircraft de-icing. Bring something to read or do while you're waiting (portable DVD players and MP3 players such as iPods are great entertainment), and pack snacks so that you'll at least be comfortable. If security regulations don't allow drinks to be brought through to the gate area of the terminal, you'll be able to buy them once you've cleared security. Also bring along your patience: it's not going to help your situation, or your travelling companions, if you're angry or impatient.

HEATED TRAVEL: WHEW!

Heat can also cause problems when you're travelling. For example, many airlines won't take pets in the cargo hold during summer periods because they may not be able to keep the hold cool enough. In some countries, heatwaves have been known to buckle train tracks, and of course the heat can cause vehicle cooling systems to fail, too. It doesn't do much for tempers either. Be aware that delays and breakdowns can happen in summer as well as winter, and be as patient as possible.

Perks and Upgrades: It's Always Worth Asking

There are definitely perks available when you travel. They include such items as category upgrades for a flight, hotel room, cruise ship cabin, or rental vehicle; free breakfasts or spa treatments; champagne or fresh fruit in your room or ship cabin on your arrival; theatre tickets... and the list goes on. The trick, of course, is having the courage to ask. But what do you have to lose? After all, the worst they can say is no. Try these strategies:

- *Book off-season.* This will allow you to take advantage of greater availability in business or first class on the airlines, as well as help you access nicer hotel accommodation at cheaper rates. Just remember that the destination may be off-season for a reason. Check up on weather and other factors that may affect your decision and your enjoyment of your vacation.

- *Ask politely.* Ask your travel agent, front desk agent, or check-in staff. You have a much better chance of being upgraded if you're pleasant, and it helps if you mention that you're celebrating a special event such as a birthday, anniversary, wedding, or graduation.

- *Dress appropriately.* Employees are more likely to upgrade you to higher levels of airline seating or nicer rooms in their hotel if you look like you belong there.

- *Do a little research.* Look for hotels that may have opened recently or cruise ships that may be launching or repositioning, because they tend to offer bonuses to those willing to try them out first.

CLAIRE'S BEST BETS FOR PLANNING FOR PARADISE

- Start your planning by setting out your travel goals, and you won't go wrong.

- Have **FUN** with your research: the Internet, books, movies—go for it!

- Build in an easy first day at your destination for maximum stress reduction.

- Apply for a passport, and use it—it's your ticket to the world.

- Understand procedures and limits for customs and immigration before you travel.

- Remember the traveller's motto: Flexible, Organized, and Prepared!

Chapter 2
Insurance: Cover Yourself!

Protecting Your Travel Investment

We all embark on trips hoping for the best, and our optimism is usually reward-ed, giving us memories that we'll always treasure. In today's travel climate, how-ever, there are hiccups that you need to be aware of and prepared for.

For example, we've all seen airline and tour companies fail, sometimes very unexpectedly and without any warning to consumers. Talk to anyone who has shown up at an airport only to find that their airplane isn't going anywhere at any time and they'll tell you that the next few hours can be chaotic and frustrating. The issue doesn't even have to be as drastic as a company's bankruptcy, though. Delays, cancellations, and illness are all common occurrences that you need to prepare yourself for, just in case. It's far better to spend some time going through worst-case scenarios before you leave rather than finding yourself unprepared if the worst happens. Consider it pragmatism rather than pessimism.

First, make sure that you use a credit card to book your travel, whether you're booking online, in person, or through a tour company or travel agent. If things go wrong, you'll be able to ask your credit card company to reverse the charge. They may ask you for some paperwork and it may take some time, but you should eventually see the charge disappear, or have your account credited. (If the charge is in dispute, the credit card company will likely not require that you pay it until the matter is dealt with.) Paying in any other way (cash, a debit card, or a cheque) gives you little recourse if the services for which you've paid aren't provided.

You also need to verify (and verify again, and again) that you know who you're dealing with, especially if you're booking travel through the Internet, but even if you're responding to ads in newspapers and magazines. There are plenty of untrustworthy websites and companies out there, so stick with those that you know are legitimate and check any others out very carefully before you give them your hard-earned money. If you decide to contact them, ask how long they've been in business, and what industry associations they belong to—and then contact the associations to ensure that they are, in fact, members. You can also call local Better Business Bureaus and provincial consumer protection agencies to find out if there have been any complaints against the company.

Insurance: Your Safety Net

I can't emphasize strongly enough the need for travel insurance. Travel can be an investment of hundreds, even thousands, of dollars. Insurance protects that investment, making sure that you'll get some, perhaps all, of it back if something goes wrong. You may believe—as many people do—that your health-care plan or credit card or household insurance will cover you if you're sick or injured, if you get into an accident with a rental car, or if your trip has to be cancelled. But read the fine print! Even if these options do give you certain coverages, they usually involve small limits and big loopholes. Please, don't rely on them. Check with health-care insurers and credit card companies so that you'll know exactly what coverage you have, and what you'll need.

Travel Best Bet!
One client booked their cruise with us, but booked their air travel by using frequent flyer points. They'd booked their return flight for 8 a.m., but were delayed on board the ship until 10 a.m. Since they'd decided against insurance coverage, they had to pay not only for a replacement flight home, but also for the two days they had to stay in a hotel before they could even get a flight out. Compare this with another client, who booked her father on a guys' international getaway of golfing and ATV riding. Three hours from the resort, her father's ATV flipped and he punctured his lung. Within 40 minutes of his travel buddies making the call to the insurance company, a Lear jet was on the tarmac, waiting to fly him home to outstanding medical care. The insurance company covered the $210,000 flight cost and medical bills—and the father made a complete recovery.

WHERE TO FIND INSURANCE

Your travel agent can recommend and provide a variety of insurance policies. Insurance agents and brokers, tour operators, airlines, cruise lines, and other travel providers also offer insurance. In addition, you'll find travel insurance policies available through your local financial institution, your auto association (or other membership-based organizations), your credit cards, and a huge range of other independent insurance providers.

The key is to understand what your needs are before you begin shopping, and then to examine each policy based on what it costs and what it provides. The cheapest alternative is definitely not always the best. In the insurance industry, you tend to get what you pay for. Remember, too, that it's essential to purchase travel insurance before you depart on the trip. Travel medical insurance can usually be purchased right up until you board a plane or cross a border out of your home country, but you need to be aware that pre-existing medical conditions may void part or all of the coverage, so it's still best to purchase this ahead of time to give yourself an opportunity to ensure that you're adequately covered. Cancellation insurance, or any package insurance that includes cancellation, typically has to be purchased within 24 to 48 hours of making a reservation.

THE ANNUAL POLICY: YOUR BEST-VALUE SECRET WEAPON

One way to reduce travel insurance costs is to consider taking out annual policies. These can offer significant cost savings compared to buying insurance before a specific trip, even if you only travel a couple of times a year.

Be aware, however, that the annual policies often have travel duration limits. For example, they may cover you for any trip that's 15 days or less. This means that you will be covered for all your trips where you are gone for 15 days or less in a given year. But you will **NOT** be covered for any days over a 15-day stay. If you do buy an annual policy for 15 days or less, but intend on taking a longer trip, all you need to do is "top-up" your insurance for the extra number of days you'll be away. So, be sure that whatever annual policy you choose, it covers all the travel that you're likely to make in the next year. You don't want to head out on a 21-day trip, for example, and discover halfway through it that your policy only covers you if you're away for 15 or fewer days.

MAKING JUDGMENTS: WHAT TO LOOK FOR IN AN INSURANCE POLICY

No matter what type of insurance you're buying, certain standard items need to be reviewed to ensure that you know exactly what's covered, when it's covered, and under what conditions it's covered. These items include the following:

- The policy's cost
- The payment terms: when and how payment is due
- The policy's term: when it starts and when it ends
- Whether it's automatically renewed

- Any deductible (an amount that you pay before insurance coverage is triggered) and how much it is
- Items that are covered, and the amount of coverage
- Exclusions, or items and conditions that aren't covered
- Whether there's a toll-free number that you need to call for pre-authorization before taking action that would result in a claim
- Procedures for making a claim against the insurance policy

PROTECTING YOUR INSURANCE INVESTMENT

If you think you have a reason to make an insurance claim, it is imperative that you call your insurance company immediately. Delaying that phone call could result in reduced coverage or even complete loss of coverage—so **DO NOT** procrastinate. You can call most insurance companies 24 hours a day, worldwide. Simply quote the policy number printed on your itinerary/invoice.

A wallet card from the insurance company with your policy number and the company's phone numbers is usually included with your policy. Keep this with you at all times. It will help avoid delays if you need to make a claim, or if you need to prove to a hospital that you have medical coverage.

Typically, all the details and the claim forms that you'll need are located inside your insurance policy booklet. You should also keep all your original receipts, because you'll need them if you incur expenses that you feel may be covered by a claim.

 Warning! Each insurance policy is different, so always read your policy carefully, including (in fact, especially) the fine print, and make sure you understand all of its clauses.

Cancellation and Interruption Insurance

Trip cancellation and interruption insurance covers you for various situations that would require you to either cancel your trip before it begins, or interrupt your trip to return home (or somewhere else) early.

 Travel Best Bet!
One of our clients was all set to travel to Mexico with her family when she was called by the courts to be a witness at a trial. Luckily, the family had purchased insurance, so although they were forced to cancel their vacation, they received a full refund from the insurance provider.

I can't tell you how many people say, "Oh, my credit card covers me for trip cancellation" when they're in my office, but once they actually look at the policy carefully they find that it doesn't offer the coverage they thought it did. If the fine print's confusing, just call your bank or the credit card's toll-free information line and ask for an explanation. Similarly, very few company benefit plans or home/auto coverages include trip cancellation.

So, why exactly do you need this coverage? Essentially, cancellation and interruption insurance covers you for non-refundable trip costs if you have to cancel or interrupt a trip for a reason that they cover. For example, they'll typically cover you if you, your travelling companion, or a close family member (check the insurer's definition of "close" family member) becomes seriously ill; if weather or mechanical problems force you to miss your flights or your cruise; if your government issues a travel warning that advises against travelling to your destination after you've purchased your ticket; if you lose your job; or if you're called for jury duty.

If you're cynical about the need for this coverage, keep in mind that it can protect you financially at a time of great emotional turmoil.

Travel Best Bet!

One client booked flights through our office to Puerto Vallarta, Mexico, to leave just three days later. He declined all insurance. The day before he was due to leave, his son tragically and unexpectedly passed away. If he had opted for cancellation insurance, it would have covered the cost of the plane tickets, which turned out to be a significant worry when the family suddenly found themselves with a number of unforeseen expenses. The last thing that you want to be concerned about at the time of a personal loss like this is the money you've just lost on a trip.

Baggage and Personal Effects Insurance

This insurance covers the cost of your baggage and its contents if your bags are damaged or (worse!) completely lost or stolen during your trip. It can help you buy replacement clothing and toiletries, and replace paperwork such as birth certificates (although you should **NEVER** put important paperwork in your checked baggage!).

If you're thinking that lost bags on an airline flight should be the airline's responsibility, you're right—to a certain extent. The airlines are supposed to pay to repair damage that they've caused, and they do provide a certain amount of re-imbursement, as per the Warsaw Convention. Compensation is based on weight, though, which is unlikely to give you anywhere close to the replacement cost of the baggage contents. Extra insurance can help you make up that difference.

Baggage loss or damage insurance claims need to be accompanied by some kind of paperwork that proves the bags actually were lost or damaged. If an airline is at the root of the problem, don't leave the airport without going to the baggage claims office to collect the airline's forms for baggage loss or damages. You'll need to describe the bags and have the airline employee ensure that all the necessary details are filled out. For more information about lost baggage, see Chapter 6, Air Travel: Flying High.

Similarly, if your bags are lost or stolen somewhere along the way—at a resort, for example—your insurance claim must usually be accompanied by a police report of lost or stolen goods. You need to have the local police prepare the report and give it directly to you, or send it to your insurance company as soon as possible after the incident occurs. Check with the insurance company's claim department before you leave the area to ensure that they've received it.

Medical Insurance

Even if you have government-funded universal health care at home (and many people around the world don't), the basic government policies don't cover you once you step outside their geographic zone. For some countries, such as Canada, that can even include a trip outside your normal province of residence. The government plan generally only reimburses you for the expenses that your medical condition would have incurred within your home area, so you could find yourself owing huge sums of money if you're hospitalized far from home. That's why travel medical insurance is absolutely essential. It covers the difference between what your government, group (through work), or private health insurance plan covers and what you're actually charged for health care when you're on the road.

Travel Best Bet!
Our agency had a group of passengers in Italy taking a fully escorted tour for most of their vacation. They booked some additional nights of independent touring as well, and organized a car rental to explore the countryside. Unfortunately, they were involved in a major car accident, and all six of them were hurt, ranging from internal injuries and broken bones to stitches and concussions. They'd taken out insurance, and so were covered for all of the medical expenses—which totalled well over $300,000.

Most travel medical insurance policies will also cover "repatriation" or "emergency evacuation" costs. This is what it costs to get you home if you're ill or injured. Medical care standards in some countries may be well below what you're used to at home, which is reason enough to fly back as soon as possible. The insurance company may want you home quickly, too, to keep costs under better control. And you'll likely feel better if you can be closer to home and your support network of family and friends. But to get you there, you may need special flights, special equipment, nursing care en route, or other costly assistance. Repatriation coverage insures you for these expenses, and often for the expenses of a travelling companion, as well. (Note that repatriation generally also includes bringing your body home if you pass away while you're on the trip.)

TRAVEL MEDICAL INSURANCE COVERAGES

You'll need to thoroughly review the insurance policy to make sure that you're covered for medical expenses. Usually any medical expense that's not related to a pre-existing condition (such as a heart condition that you know about) will be covered, with most travel medical insurance plans not requiring you to undergo insurance medicals. These expenses usually include emergency medical and dental treatment, ambulance fees, prescription drugs needed to treat you for a sudden illness or medical emergency, and the cost of getting you home or getting a family member to your bedside.

If you have pre-existing conditions that could flare up while you're travelling (such as angina, for example), you'll need a more robust travel medical insurance policy. You can expect this to be considerably more expensive than a regular plan, and you may need a medical examination in order to qualify for the insurance, as well.

Whether or not you have pre-existing conditions, be sure to read—and understand—the small print, especially the details about exclusion clauses (there's often a clause that denies coverage for any alcohol-related injuries, for example).

UNDERSTANDING THE LANGUAGE OF MEDICAL INSURANCE

Medical insurance policies frequently use terms such as "stable" and "pre-existing" conditions. You need to check the fine print on your policy very carefully and then discuss it with your insurance agent. A pre-existing condition is something like a heart condition or diabetes. If you have a heart condition, and subsequently suffer a heart attack while you're away, your policy may or may not cover you. That's why it's so important to understand the language, and to declare any conditions that you have when you take out the policy. If you leave out the fact that you have a heart condition, trust me, the insurance company **WILL** find out, and they **WILL** deny you coverage for that heart attack.

DON'T FORGET! MEDICAL TRAVEL INSURANCE FOR SHORT TRIPS

It doesn't matter how long or short your trip is, the most important thing is where you're going. People have "popped across the border" between Canada and the United States for a quick trip, only to be involved in an accident or fall ill in the foreign country, with the added horror of discovering that they're facing serious medical expenses.

Travel Best Bet!
One woman with whom I worked (who was a seasoned travel consultant at the time) was travelling with her mother to New York. Because they lived in Vancouver, British Columbia, which is located close to the border with the United States, she found a cheap flight leaving from Seattle, Washington, and was willing to drive the 2.5 hours to take advantage of it. Knowing that she and her mother would be crossing the border, she covered them both with Deluxe Package Insurance. What she failed to do was think about covering her father, who drove them to the airport in Seattle. He had a serious car accident on the way home after dropping them off and had to be hospitalized for three days. It cost them over $20,000.

Let's put this into perspective. The cost of travel medical insurance for someone 59 years and under is typically less than $5 per day. I've seen bills for tens of thousands of dollars for people who needed to be hospitalized for just one night in a foreign country. Imagine if you had to stay longer or needed major surgery. Yikes!

Wherever you're travelling, but especially if you're crossing a border, double-check that you have the right travel medical insurance. It really is worth it.

Avoiding Disaster: Does a Travel Warning Void Your Travel Insurance?

Disasters such as earthquakes and tsunamis and sudden political unrest tend to attract the attention of travellers pretty quickly. The prospect of losing possessions, and even loved ones, hits close to home. This highlights the importance and value of travel insurance. It's essential not only to obtain appropriate insurance before travelling, but to understand the implications of government-issued "travel warnings" on that coverage, whether they're issued due to political unrest or a recent natural disaster.

If you book travel to a country or a region after the government has issued a travel warning, your travel insurance typically excludes coverage. But if you already had plans to travel to the afflicted areas—and you purchased your trip and insurance before the warning was issued—your travel insurance should protect you if you decide to cancel your trip.

You should always consult a qualified travel or insurance agent, and check your government's foreign affairs department website for updated travel warnings before booking and again before travelling.

Rescue Me: When You Need More Than Insurance

If you're travelling for long periods, especially in areas of political or economic unrest, you may need something more than insurance policies designed for vacation travel. A number of security companies now offer a variety of services that include travel insurance policies, but at a premium level of service. They also provide pre-trip and en-route advice, security as necessary, emergency evacuation for non-medical reasons, their own medical staff or clinics in various global locations, and other services. They do cost more, but if your circumstances warrant it, they could be invaluable.

Cutting through the Red Tape: Making a Claim

The most important thing to remember when making a claim on any insurance policy is to first check the insurance policy's claim procedures. Not following the company's process, or not including all the requested information, can result in your claim being denied. Pay particular attention to any time restrictions that the policy has for making claims. It doesn't matter how valid your claim is if you miss the deadline for filing it.

As I mentioned earlier, it's essential to phone the insurance company as soon as you believe you need to make a claim, especially if medical treatment is needed. They can pre-certify the treatment, which in some cases can allow the medical-care provider to bill the insurance company directly, rather than having you pay the expenses and wait for reimbursement. In some cases, pre-certification is a necessary part of authorizing the claim. If you don't pre-certify, your claim may be denied completely.

Keep all the receipts and paperwork related to your claim. If you have to submit them via traditional mail make sure that you keep photocopies on file before you send off the package, and ensure that you send it as registered mail or via a courier service to keep it as safe as possible.

If you have any questions when you're filling out claim forms, simply call the insurance company. Note down when you called and who you spoke to, along with their answers to your questions in case you need to explain the process later. They'll likely give you a file reference number that you should keep handy to minimize the number of times you need to repeat the same information.

Even if your claim is denied, that may not be the end of the process. Find out what appeal process your insurance company has, and if your local, regional, or national government has some kind of ombudsman's office that may be able to help you out. Your travel agent can often point you in the right direction.

CLAIRE'S BEST BETS FOR INSURANCE

- The insurance bottom line: **BUY IT!!**

- Buy insurance at the same time you are booking and paying for your trip.

- If you think you need to make a claim, call the insurance policy's toll-free number immediately. Unless it's a medical emergency, the insurance company can legally deny your claim if they don't receive notification about what's happening.

- Keep all your receipts. You'll need them if you need to make a claim.

- When making a claim, follow the insurance company's procedures to the letter.

- Read the fine print. Twice.

Chapter 3
Ready... Set... Prepare!

A Little Preparation Goes a Long Way

Modern life is often incredibly busy. For many of us, a vacation is something to anticipate with pleasure—a real treat to look forward to, whether it's a warm-weather getaway from winter or a summer road trip with the family. Of course, you want to make the most out of every minute of your vacation, from relaxing on the beach to touring Britain's historic castles and stately homes.

The secret to maximizing your trip's potential for relaxation or exploration lies in being prepared. But over the years I've heard numerous stories from frustrated travellers who've had to spend precious moments of their vacations fixing problems—problems that would never have arisen had they taken the time to plan properly before beginning their vacation. The old cliché about an ounce of prevention being worth a pound of cure is definitely appropriate in this case. Proper preparation is your best defence against the unexpected.

Itineraries: Putting Time on Your Side

You don't need to plan your schedule down to the last second—and if you truly prefer to travel on the spur of the moment, not making plans for hotel rooms until you're in your destination airport, for example, then far be it from me to try to dissuade you. In fact, some airports even have hotel boards or booking services that make this relatively painless. Of course, spontaneity also requires flexibility and a good measure of pragmatism. That gorgeous beachfront cottage you see in the travel magazine may not—in fact, most probably will not—be available when you arrive at your destination! But you know, people do cancel, so who knows what may be available at the last minute?

All travellers, however, regardless of whether they're laid-back and spontaneous or organized and detail oriented, need an itinerary for their vacation. Putting together a single comprehensive itinerary that contains details of your travel plans will be invaluable not just for you when you're away from home, but also for your friends and family who are holding the fort while you're away.

Before you depart, an itinerary allows you to identify deficiencies in your planning that would not otherwise reveal themselves until you're at your destination (at which point, of course, it's too late for preventive measures). And once you're on the road it becomes an excellent source for all your key phone numbers and directions. If you leave a copy with a friend or family member it could help them if they need to reach you in an emergency, or even pick you up at the airport. An added benefit of leaving a copy of your itinerary with a trusted friend or family member is that if you lose the copy you have with you, you've got a backup. An electronic version could be with you in minutes!

It's best to organize itineraries chronologically. Start with your flights or other travel arrangements, and add in your hotels and other accommodation, night by night. Include whatever key details you have: flight numbers; booking confirmation numbers; hotel names, addresses, phone and fax numbers, and e-mail and Internet addresses; and your travel agent's contact information (if there's a problem, sometimes one phone call back home can be enough to sort it out). It's also a very good idea to keep the following information with your itinerary: traveller's cheque serial numbers and photocopies of your passports, insurance policies, credit cards (back and front), and any other key identification. Keeping yourself organized in this way will make your life much easier if any of your important documents go missing. (Just remember to keep these copies separate from the original documents.)

Currency: Show Me the Money! $ £ ¢ ¥ €

If I had to pick one issue that causes the most stress for travellers it would be money! How much? Which currencies? Where can I get cash? Can I use a credit card?

These are all justifiable concerns. With a little thought before you go, however, you can alleviate or at least reduce the stress associated with money issues. In most cases, the answers to your questions will depend on where you're going and how you're getting there.

CASH: HOW MUCH IS ENOUGH?

No matter where you're going, it's always advisable to take some local currency with you. Your first challenge is to determine how much, and that depends very much on your situation. Will you be hungry or thirsty when you arrive? (Check your flight times to help you with this one.) Will you need money for a taxi to your hotel? How easy will it be to obtain cash? To use a credit card? To redeem traveller's cheques? You need to consider all possible arrival expenses.

This includes costs related to where you are staying. If you're transferring to an all-inclusive resort, you probably won't need lots of local currency, although it's a good idea to have enough for a taxi, just in case your transfer doesn't show up as promised. If, on the other hand, you're staying at a self-catering cottage and you need to buy groceries on arrival, you'll need more cash. For most trips, though, you'll only want enough local cash upon arrival to pay for the first couple of days' worth of meals, transport, and sundry expenses such as tips for hotel staff. Since credit and debit cards are less accepted in some countries outside North America, you may need more cash than you'd usually carry on you at home.

There's also a final consideration: what if something goes wrong? Think of the worst-case scenario: what if you misplace your traveller's cheques or lose your wallet? These aren't things we like to think about, but proper planning can minimize the time you have to spend dealing with them. (This is why it's a good idea to keep your cash divided up in more than one place, so that you don't lose it all if, for example, your wallet goes missing.)

Obviously, you want to strike a balance between convenience (not having to run to the bank or ATM every day for more cash) and security (not carrying around large sums of local cash). Think about the country you're going to, as well. If you're going somewhere off the beaten path, and their local currency isn't easily available, you may want to carry your cash in an alternative currency that's acceptable there. US dollars are often accepted in other countries and may also be more easily exchanged for local currency at your destination's banks.

EXCHANGING MONEY: AM I PAYING TOO MUCH?

I generally suggest to people that they not worry too much about whether they're getting the absolute best possible exchange rate. The difference between the best rate and a decent rate is probably only a few dollars, and settling for the decent rate can save you time that you'd otherwise spend hunting down the best rate. If you know well in advance of your trip that you'll need the foreign currency, though, keep an eye on the rates. If it looks like they're moving in a more expensive direction, you may want to start buying your foreign currency sooner rather than later.

Your biggest savings will likely be in advance at your own bank or local currency exchange bureau, or at your destination through an ATM. Most ATMs use a wholesale interbank exchange rate, which is two to seven percent better than what you'd get by converting Canadian dollars at an airport, an exchange counter, or even a bank. However, before you leave, do check with your financial institution about how much you can expect to pay for international withdrawals. Airport currency exchanges may not give you the best rate, but they win out on convenience. Whatever you do, avoid the black-market money-changers that you'll find in less developed areas. You can't guarantee that you're receiving a good rate, or even that you're receiving legitimate currency in some cases.

If you're travelling to a country where the inflation rate is very high, and where the value of the currency and prices in stores can vary quite a bit from day to day, you're best advised to exchange smaller amounts of money daily or every couple of days. Otherwise you could find that the money you exchanged at the beginning of the trip is worth much less by the end of it.

The biggest mistake people usually make is exchanging too much money, and losing when they exchange the money back into their home currency. Again, try to strike a balance between having sufficient cash on hand for the expenses you anticipate, and not having so much that you'll have to exchange large quantities back into your own currency when you get home. For a good Internet guide to currency conversion, check out www.xe.com.

HOW WILL YOU BE PAYING: CREDIT CARD, CASH, DEBIT, OR TRAVELLER'S CHEQUE?

Credit Cards

In many areas of the world, you just can't beat the convenience of a credit card. In particular, not just an American Express or Diner's Card, but a more widely accepted card such as Visa or MasterCard. However, there are a few things you should do prior to departing to avoid any credit card hassles while you're away.

- *Credit Limits: Have I got room?* Check your limit. If the card is nearly maxed out, or has a low limit, you'll need to compensate by having more cash and traveller's cheques to back you up. If you have more than one credit card with good limits, you won't be as dependent upon cash and traveller's cheques. If your limit is low, you can deposit money into the card before you go to increase your available credit.

- *Expiry Dates: What do you mean I can't use this card?* I've heard this story more than once from stressed out and embarrassed travellers. "Oops, my card expired when I was away and I couldn't use it." It only takes a second to check the expiry date on your credit card before you leave, and it can save hours of hassle and frustration.

- *Fraud Protection: It's for your own good, really!* Be sure to call your credit card provider's toll-free lines before you leave to let them know that you'll be travelling. The providers have excellent transaction monitoring abilities, and they'll likely notice if more purchases than usual are being made, or if the card's being used outside its normal geographic area. Many companies will then attempt to contact you by phone to ensure that the purchases are egitimate and that the card hasn't been stolen. If they can't reach you, they may suspend the card, meaning that you suddenly—and more crucially, with no warning whatsoever—won't be able to use it.

- *Nuts and Bolts.* Before you leave, be sure to ask your credit card provider how much you'll be charged if you withdraw cash from your card while you're away and what the exchange rate is likely to be. If you're travelling for several months, set yourself up with Internet banking so that you'll be able to pay your credit card bills while you're away, or set up automatic direct debits to pay down your card each month. Like ATM withdrawals, credit card purchases are also changed at the interbank rate. But beware! Credit card companies can levy fees for purchases made abroad. Their rates vary, so do your homework.

Automated Teller Machines and Debit Cards

Over the years, there has been a real trend towards people using debit cards instead of carrying cash. When you're on vacation you'll find Interac-equipped ATMs in most developed destinations and urban areas, but in many other areas, you may be out of luck. Debit cards are very popular in Canada, Britain, and the United States, but they're not as widely used elsewhere. Before you leave, check which network your card belongs to (e.g., Plus, Exchange, or Cirrus), so that you can recognize which ATM machine you can use. And remember that your financial institution may set daily limits on how much you can withdraw. Keep in mind, too, that some international ATMs only accept four-digit PINs, so if yours is longer, change it before you leave!

The downside of using ATMs is the ever-increasing fees imposed by both your bank and the ATM. Many banks charge a flat US$3 to US$5 for each visit to a cash machine overseas, in addition to the local bank's fee. If you plan to rely on ATMs abroad, shop around for banks with minimal charges. Fees are typically listed on bank websites. Some bank customers can avoid all access fees by using ATMs at select banks abroad. If you can't avoid fees then I recommend estimating your expenses and making a single withdrawal. Just keep the money safe and spend it before you return so you don't have to change it back to dollars.

Also, before heading to countries that don't attract many tourists, be sure to obtain some foreign money. If there isn't a functioning ATM or exchange counter open at the airport, you'll at least have cash to pay for a taxi. You can order currency through banks or on websites like Direct FX at www.foreign-currency.com.

Traveller's Cheques and Cheque Cards

Although traveller's cheques aren't as popular as they once were, they can still come in very handy. It's vital, though, that you take note of the serial numbers and keep them in a separate location from the cheques themselves. Before you sign the second signature on the cheque (which makes them legal tender), double-check that the store or restaurant actually accepts traveller's cheques and sign only in front of the person who is accepting them as payment.

One fantastic new development is a traveller's cheque card that you can load with money in currencies such as dollars, euros, or pounds. You can use it virtually anywhere that credit cards are accepted (but only to its prepaid limit), and if it's stolen, the money left on the card is refundable. Plus, it provides a little bit more security because, unlike a debit card, it's not linked to a specific bank account.

My Advice: Take a Bit of Everything!

The best plan is to mix up your money. Make sure that you have some local currency, some traveller's cheques, and your ATM card, plus a well-known credit card like Visa or MasterCard. Of course, researching standard practices at your destination will help. Find out ahead of time what's most acceptable there, and adapt your plans accordingly.

Electrical Current: Don't Be Shocked!

Some travellers prefer to use their own favourite electrical appliances, like a razor or hair dryer. I personally won't travel anywhere without my favourite curling iron! However, I have to warn you that some of those favourite appliances end up not coming home again, usually because their owners didn't look into the different voltage or plug requirements of the destination they're visiting.

> **TBB** *Travel Best Bet!*
> *A very close friend of mine—a smart, university-educated woman—took her favourite flat iron on vacation. The iron plug's prongs fit into the wall outlet just fine, so she plugged it in to heat up while she washed her hair. Ten minutes later, she was horrified to find that her flat iron was totally "fried." She learned the hard way that just because the plug fits in the wall outlet, it doesn't mean the voltage is compatible.*

To solve this potentially hazardous problem, there are two important factors to consider: voltage conversion and plug style (some voltage converters come with plug adapters, making life much easier).

When the voltage is different from that of your home country, you'll need to take appliances that are either automatically dual-voltage (many computer devices such as laptops, for example, have a built-in feature that automatically detects either 110V or 220V—check your owner's manual or the serial number plate on the laptop, or call the manufacturer), or appliances that can be switched back and forth (such as hair dryers). But first, find out which appliances you'll really need. Many hotels include a hair dryer in the bathroom, along with dual plugs for North American electric razors. Again, doing your research can save you time and aggravation (and precious space in your suitcase).

If you want to take an appliance with you that is not dual voltage, you'll need a voltage converter (used by North Americans travelling in Europe, for example, to go from 220V in the wall down to 110V at the appliance, or by Europeans to reverse the process). This is a one-time investment that's worthwhile if you're planning more foreign travel in the future. Think ahead about the most heavy-duty electrical appliance with which you're likely to travel, and choose your voltage converter accordingly. Most travel converters will be just fine for electric razors or hair dryers.

Once you've properly sorted out the voltage of your appliance, your next consideration is to ensure that the plug will fit into the wall outlets at your destination. All sorts of different types of plugs are used throughout the world: two- or three-pronged, and round, flat, or square plugs. As long as your voltage is okay, all you need for your appliance is an adapter to change your appliance's plug into a form that the outlets at your destination will accept. These are very inexpensive and are widely available at travel stores (and airports, if you forget!).

Hands Off! Protecting Your Home While You're Away

As most police services and insurance companies will tell you, when the home-owner's away, the mice—or the thieves—will play. Do everything that you can to make your home appear lived in and completely "business as usual" while you're on vacation:

- Don't change your answering machine or voicemail message at home to one that says you're away—that's like advertising that your home is unoccupied.

- Test your smoke detector to make sure that it's working.

- Several days before you leave, check all doors and windows to make sure that they lock.

- Ask a neighbour or hire a service to keep up with outdoor jobs such as mowing, raking leaves, or shovelling snow. An unkempt yard also advertises that your home may be unoccupied.

- Cancel newspaper and mail delivery (this includes delivery to a community mailbox), preferably with a start date a few days before you leave, so that you can verify the cancellation. Ask a friend or neighbour to keep an eye out for stray papers and mail, including advertising flyers. If you travel regularly, consider posting a sign on your door refusing all flyers so that delivery personnel get used to not leaving flyers at your door.

- Use variable timers to turn on lights and a radio at different times each day. When you're setting your timers, keep in mind that you're trying to mimic your normal activity as far as possible, so you might have lights turn on in a bedroom in the evening right after they turn off in a living room.

- Turn off appliances such as computers, VCRs, and microwave ovens (unplugging these appliances also protects them from power surges during electrical storms). If a valuable item can be seen through the windows, either move it or close the window coverings.

- Shut off the water supply to your clothes washer: the supply hoses are notorious for bursting, which can create major water damage if you're not home.

- If you're on a well instead of city water, check before you leave that the cap over the well is in good condition and locked. This ensures that nothing can get into the well while you're gone, from groundwater runoff to small children exploring where they shouldn't. You should also switch off your pump.

- You can lower the thermostat to save on heating bills while you're gone, but make sure that the house stays warm enough that there's absolutely no risk of frozen pipes during cold weather. Your home insurance policy also likely requires that someone check the house daily during cold weather to ensure that any heating problems are caught as quickly as possible. Read the fine print. (That should be second nature to you by this stage.)

- Ask a neighbour to put out and take in your garbage can or recycling boxes on the appropriate day. Remember that you want everything to look as it does when you're at home.

- Unplug your garage door opener or switch off its electrical circuit so that it won't open accidentally (or in case a thief attempts to use a remote opener on it).

- Leave your itinerary with someone you trust so that you can be reached in an emergency.

- Ensure that you have an inventory list (written or in the form of photos or videos) of all the items in your home, and store it off-site somewhere so that you can identify what's missing if necessary. Also ensure that valuables are marked with an engraving pen or other identifier, or—even better—move them to a safety deposit box if that's practical.

- Ensure that important documents, such as home insurance policies, are either stored off-site in a safety deposit box or on-site in a fire-rated container (these are easily obtainable from office supply stores). Don't rely on folk tales such as storing paperwork in the freezer—despite their insulation, freezers do burn.

- Remove your registration information and insurance from your vehicle, especially if it's left parked at the airport.

Baggage: Don't Let It Weigh You Down

Luggage options these days are endless. You can almost literally find any size, shape, colour, and material you can think of. With all these choices, figuring out the right bag for your trip can be a bit tricky.

Start by determining how long you'll be away. This will determine the size of bag you'll need. You obviously won't need a huge suitcase if you're going for a weekend in Las Vegas, but you'll need to go bigger for a three-week African safari. Opt for the smallest size that will comfortably get you there, and keep in mind that—thanks to laundry facilities on the road—you can probably travel pretty well for several months on the same wardrobe that will handle just a couple of weeks. Try to aim for a 16- or 18-inch (40 or 45 cm) suitcase for weekend trips, and a 22-inch (55 cm) suitcase for longer trips. The larger 26-inch (66 cm) suitcases look attractive in terms of space, but they can be awkward to manoeuvre in tight spaces such as trains, and it's very easy to pack too much into them, making them too heavy. Airlines are currently reducing the size and weight limits of luggage that passengers are allowed to take free of charge so a heavy bag could mean you pay a heavy price! Be sure to check the airline's baggage restrictions—both weight and height—before you pack. These restrictions are usually printed on your ticket.

Look at the activities you intend to do while you're away. If you're going on a shopping trip, you'll need to leave room for purchases you make. Likewise, if you are travelling over the holidays, you may need to make room for gifts you are taking to family and to bring home any gifts you may receive while you're away.

Also consider how you're travelling. Hard-sided luggage can be heavy, for example, but it's also sturdy and can protect its contents better than soft-sided luggage. If you have to carry your luggage many times throughout your trip, the convenience factor will become more important. Bags with wheels are my absolute favourite travel invention ever, but the wheels can be damaged in transit. It's best to choose bags with recessed wheels, because their design limits their vulnerability in baggage handling systems.

If you're planning an active vacation or taking a number of different forms of transportation, consider a backpack that converts into a wheeled suitcase. It's slightly heavier than a conventional backpack, but it offers you the convenience of carrying the load over your shoulders when wheeling it isn't an option.

Personal style is a consideration for many people when choosing their bags. That's why I have a pink carry-on bag! But you need to be realistic. Bags get chewed up and banged up during travel, and the expensive ones are often damaged more easily than cheaper ones (and they can be a bigger target for theft, too). Go with lightweight bags to avoid using up half your luggage weight allowance with the suitcase before you even put any clothes in it. Nylon with a denier of at least 430 is a good choice because it's very tough without being very heavy and it comes in a lot of colours. Including pink!

Corners and handles tend to get damaged easily, so check that they're reinforced and that there's no loose stitching anywhere that could be snagged. Check zippers to make sure that they operate smoothly, with no rough spots. Bag handles and shoulder straps should be cushioned for comfort. Pockets are useful for keeping items separated and organized, but again should be securely stitched.

MY BAGS ARE WHERE? SECURING YOUR BAGS

While there are no guarantees that your bags will arrive safely, there are certainly ways to improve the odds. Make sure that each bag is clearly labelled—inside and out—with your name. For security reasons it's not a good idea to use your home address. Use a post office box number or your work address instead. It's also not a good idea to have your destination address showing, as it potentially lets people know where you'll be, which can enable them to find out additional information about you. I recommend using a luggage tag with a flap that conceals your personal details from the public.

You should also secure all your luggage straps. Take off any removable shoulder or other straps and tuck them inside one of the exterior pockets or in your carry-on bag (to keep them handy when you get to your destination), as dangling straps can get caught in baggage handling machinery.

SECURING LUGGAGE: CAN I USE A LOCK?

At one time I advised securing each bag with a sturdy lock and keeping the keys safe in your carry-on bag, purse, or wallet. However, new security procedures in some airports won't let you put locks on your bags in case they need to be opened and examined between the time that you check them in and when they're loaded on the plane.

One way to solve that problem is to use a lock that allows US Transportation Security Administration (TSA) access with a universal key. When you're looking to purchase one of these locks, it must be identified as "approved by TSA." All other locks will be cut off to allow the inspectors access.

If you're not using a TSA-approved lock, you could secure the zippers or fasteners on your bag with a sturdy plastic twist tie or recloseable plastic tie, just to keep the zippers from opening up.

ALL THESE BAGS LOOK ALIKE! IDENTIFYING YOUR BAG

To help you identify your suitcase among hundreds of others on airport conveyer belts, use ribbon or bright (and sturdy) luggage tags attached to the handles. It's also not a bad idea to cinch a luggage strap around the suitcase. It helps as an identifier, and also gives the suitcase some support in case a zipper or buckle breaks.

Since so many bags look alike, I recommend taking a photo of your suitcase before you leave and tucking the photo into your carry-on bag. It sounds a little crazy, but if your luggage goes missing, you'll be asked for a description, and it's amazing how difficult it is to remember what it looked like!

WHAT HAPPENS TO MY BAGS IF I HAVE CONNECTING FLIGHTS?

Most of the time, your bags can be checked right through to your final destination, even if you're taking several connecting flights. However, if you're travelling through different countries on those flights, or with several different airlines, it may not be quite so simple. Be sure to ask at check-in whether your bags are automatically transferred between your flights, or whether you'll have to pick them up yourself.

If you have to clear customs at a stopover airport, you'll probably need to pick up your luggage, clear it through customs, and then drop it back onto a conveyer belt that will take it to your next airplane. Just check with airline personnel at check-in (and at arrival at your stopover airport if you're concerned) to find out whether you'll need to do this. Don't be afraid to ask if you're unsure about something.

Making the Most of the Space You Have: The Art of Packing

For many people, packing can be a real nightmare. And, indeed, it can be tough to narrow down an entire wardrobe of choices to a weekend or a week's worth of clothes, especially when luggage space and weight are considerations. The trick is to make sure that you have everything you need in a small and convenient bag, weighing as little as possible. Easier said than done, I know, but it is possible!

BAGGAGE LIMITS: THE AIRLINES ARE SERIOUS

Before you choose which bag to take or start packing anything in it, it's essential to look into the baggage limits of the airline you are flying. If you take a bag that's oversize or overweight it could end up costing you dearly. Baggage size and weight limits should be printed on your tickets. If they aren't, they'll certainly be available on the airline's website. You must double-check the restrictions before you finalize your packing.

Most airlines restrict you to two pieces of checked baggage, neither of which can weigh more than 50 lb (23 kg) per piece, and many airlines limit you to even less than this. Considering that excess baggage charges can be extremely hefty, it's wise to keep within your limits. The airlines don't always check the weight, but if they do, you could pay a lot of extra money.

 Travel Best Bet!
One colleague of mine found herself repacking her two pieces of checked baggage at the airline check-in counter, in full view of the line-up of people behind her. One of her suitcases was overweight, so she had to transfer some heavier items to the other case in order to have her luggage accepted by the airline. It wasn't the best start to her trip!

You're usually permitted one carry-on bag that will fit below the seat in front of you, or in the overhead compartment. Airlines restrict the size of this bag and most have a special frame at their check-in counters that the bag has to fit into in order to be allowed on board. You're also restricted in terms of what you can carry in that bag, but it's tough to keep up with what's allowed and what's not, especially as this can change at short notice due to security issues, and may vary in different countries. Check your airline's website or toll-free number before you go to make sure that you have the latest information. You'll also need to check the security regulations at the airports you'll be travelling through. If higher security alerts are in effect, you may be further restricted in the size, contents, and type of items you can put into your carry-on luggage.

If you're carrying luggage that's a little out of the ordinary, such as sporting equipment or large containers, check with the airline before you arrive at the airport so that you'll know what to expect at the check-in counter. You may need special boxes for bicycles, for example.

Travel Best Bet!
Many of our clients usually travel with regular, sched-uled airlines, which typically have larger luggage lim-its than charter airlines. If they haven't checked the luggage limits indicated on their documentation when they're travelling by charter, some have had to pay some hefty fees in both directions, because they've assumed that the limits are higher than they really are. Make sure you factor in the limit for your return trip, too, if you expect to purchase a lot of items while you're away.

WHAT WILL I WEAR? FIGURING OUT THE "MUST-BRING" LIST

To figure out what you need to take with you, start by looking at your itinerary. Make a list of your activities each day, and the clothes and other items that you'll need. For example, if you're on a cruise and you have a shore day that includes a walking tour of a historic city in the morning, sea kayaking in the afternoon, and a sit-down dinner in the evening, you'll want one comfortable, sporty outfit that will take you from walking to kayaking (perhaps you can wear a two-piece swim-suit under your walking shorts and top), and one smarter outfit for dinner.

Once you've listed the outfits you'll need each day, start making a list of the clothes you can take to build those outfits. Keep to one colour scheme if you can (using neutrals such as blue, brown, or black as a theme often works well) to achieve maximum "mixing and matching" of individual pieces. If you take washable clothes (rather than dry-clean-only), you can handwash items to get even more mileage out of them. Choose accessories, including shoes (which are well-known suitcase space stealers), the same way, to go with as many outfits as possible.

PACKING TOILETRIES: MAKING A LIST AND CHECKING IT TWICE

The easiest way to pack toiletries is to pay close attention as you go through your usual morning and evening routines a week or so in advance of your departure. Make a list of everything that you use, so that you won't forget anything essential when you're packing.

If space and weight are a consideration, travel-size containers are wonderful inventions. Items such as reduced-size toiletries, a small hair dryer, and fold-away rain gear that you only use for travelling can be handily stored in one place in your closet or drawers, perhaps in their own bag or box—then you won't have to hunt all over the house for them when you're packing. Most hotels will have a sundries store, but don't count on them having your favourite face cream, hair conditioner, or toothpaste. If you can't live without it, don't forget to pack it, especially if you're travelling outside North America, where your regular brands and variety may be limited.

 Travel Best Bet!
A client of ours with blonde hair forgot to pack hair con-
ditioner when she travelled to Cuba, and couldn't find
it anywhere after her arrival. She came back with light
green hair, the result of swimming in chlorinated water
with unprotected bleached hair. Not the best look in
vacation photos!

WHAT GOES WHERE? PACKING A CARRY-ON BAG

Gather together everything on your "must-bring" list a few days before your departure, and separate it out into carry-on bag and checked luggage categories. Carry-on items should include anything that you'll need both on the way to your destination and for the first day there in case your checked luggage doesn't arrive on time. Carry-on bags are also the place for valuables, although you should limit those as much as possible when you're travelling.

I used to recommend that an extra shirt or blouse and underwear, plus toiletries and items to pass the time en route, were essential. However, with new carry-on luggage security restrictions, you may not be able to include anything that comes in a gel or a liquid, such as shampoos and even toothpaste, or you may be restricted to smaller sizes. Be sure to check your airline's website for the current rules before you pack. Consider packing toiletries in your checked luggage, especially if they're in larger sizes. To get you through your journey you can still take a toothbrush, and you should be able to include breath mints (or "strips" that melt on your tongue) and pre-moistened facial and hand wipes. You may be able to purchase toiletries after you've cleared security, but they'll likely be more expensive than at your local store, and if you need to clear security again (if you're transferring to an international flight, for example), you'll run into the same restrictions.

Pack just the essentials in your carry-on bag: travel documents such as passports and tickets, house and car keys, cellphone, money, camera, clearly labelled prescription medicines (see also Chapter 4, Staying Healthy, for more on taking medication with you), an extra sweater in case the plane is chilly, and photos of your checked luggage and a contents list in case it gets lost. (For detailed packing lists, see the checklists at the end of the book.)

FITTING IT ALL IN: PACKING YOUR SUITCASE

Some people find it difficult to organize and decide what they need to take on a trip. For others, it's "fitting it all in" that's the hard part. There are some fool-proof tips, however, to help you perfect the art of packing your bags.

- Heavy or large items should go at the bottom of the suitcase (nearest the wheels). This includes shoes, hair dryer and travel iron, but leave the hair dryer and iron at home if you know your hotel offers them. This gives them some protection in case the bag is knocked about or dropped, and also keeps the weight down low and the suitcase centred, helping it avoid a tendency to tip over.

- Avoid packing easily broken items. If you can't avoid it, wrap them in socks or sweaters, and put them in the centre of the case where they'll be buffered by more clothing.

- Use all the space you have, including space inside shoes: stuffing them with socks or underwear saves room, and also protects the shoe from being crushed.

- Preventing wrinkles is always a challenge, but it can help to put tissue paper or plastic dry-cleaning bags between layers of clothes. Rolling your clothes, instead of folding them, can also help. Or, try laying your longest items, such as dresses or pants, into your case, so that the excess drapes over the suitcase edges. Add shirts and skirts that fit into the case on top, and then fold over the excess from the longer items.

- Carry resealable plastic bags, such as freezer bags, for keeping wet clothing and spillable items away from everything else in your suitcase.

- Put whatever you'll need first, such as sleepwear, on top, where it will be easy to reach quickly.

- Choose to wear bulky clothing or shoes en route if you're having trouble fitting them into your suitcase.

- If you're travelling with family members, it's best for each person to have their own checked bag, but consider tucking an outfit from one person into another person's case. That way, if someone's luggage gets lost, they'll have at least one outfit in addition to what they're wearing and what's in their carry-on bag.

Once your luggage is packed, use the "lift" test to ensure that you haven't over-loaded yourself. Imagine that you're at an airport or train station, and that you can't find any available porters or luggage carts. Put your carry-on bag over your shoulder and lift up your checked luggage. Can you comfortably lift the suitcase onto an airline conveyer belt? And, using the wheels on your luggage, can you transport everything through the airport or train terminal? The best rule of packing is to never travel with more than you can carry by yourself.

WHERE DO I SAFELY PACK FILM?

Storing camera film in your checked luggage used to be the best way to protect it, but with the stronger security X-ray devices currently in use, your undeveloped photo or slide film will definitely be damaged. Put it in carry-on bags: the walk-through and hand-wand security devices of most developed countries won't affect most film at 800 ISO or lower, although they can damage film of any speed if the film is exposed to them more than five times.

If you're concerned, you can ask for your film to be hand-inspected to avoid the X-rays, but be aware that security regulations may not allow this in all countries. You can also buy special cases designed for protecting film, but security personnel may consider these suspicious, and you'll likely end up with a physical inspection of your bags so that they can see what the security machines can't.

You can try mailing the film home to yourself, but this may be even riskier than airport security, depending on where you're travelling. Screening equipment doesn't affect digital camera images or processed film or slides, so this may be the ideal time to go digital.

 Travel Best Bet!
We had a family on a once-in-a-lifetime trip to Disney-land who'd gone all out, stayed at the Grand Californian, and taken tons of pictures. They put their film into their checked luggage—and were horrified once they arrived home and developed the pictures to find that the film had been ruined by the high-tech scanning devices now used at the airport.

Travel Funnies

After thousands of calls from people, the lack of awareness that many people have with respect to travelling never fails to amaze. I suppose that it compelled me, in part, to write this book. To lighten your planning, here are a few of the funniest moments I've experienced over the years:

- A call asking for advice on how to handle the man who wanted to ride inside the kennel with his dog so he wouldn't have to pay for a seat.

- A woman wanting to know why she had to change clothes on her flight between Vancouver and Miami (she was told she'd have to make a change between the two cities).

- Calls from people not knowing how to spell the name of their own city.

- A woman thinking she needed to have a passport to fly between Winnipeg and Toronto.

- A client asking whether an "outbound flight" meant that it was arriving or departing.

- Many calls from adults who don't know the difference between a.m. and p.m.!

- A client thinking that a connecting flight meant the plane sticks to something.

- A woman asking for an aisle seat in the aircraft so that her hair wouldn't get messed up by being near the window.

- A client becoming irate because he was told that he couldn't rent a car to drive between Honolulu and Maui.

- A client who was told she needed a visa to travel to China responding with "Oh dear, I only have a MasterCard."

CLAIRE'S BEST BETS FOR READY… SET… PREPARE!

- Putting together a written itinerary helps you keep all the travel details together—and it gives those at home an easy way to reach you if needed.

- When it comes to money, take a little of everything: cash, traveller's cheques, debit cards, and credit cards.

- Check which electrical current your destination uses to avoid frying your hair dryer!

- Don't forget to take security precautions for your home before you leave.

- When it comes to packing, keep one cardinal rule in mind: go light!!

Chapter 4
Staying Healthy

Healthy Travel Starts at Home

Even travelling within your own country can play all kinds of tricks on your system. Your daily routine, your sleeping patterns, and your diet all change. For some of us, that's all it takes for our bodies to rebel, often in the form of mild digestive upsets or headaches. A day or two of taking it easy, though, and we're back in top form.

There are some serious health hazards associated with travel, however, from food poisoning to tropical diseases. But the vast majority of these are avoidable if you take a few sensible precautions, keeping in mind where you're travelling. An all-inclusive tropical resort may, of course, offer far fewer risks than an adventure trip through a remote jungle, but don't take this for granted.

One of the most important precautions you can take is to make sure that you're as healthy as possible before you travel. Whether or not you need a physical exam before the trip will depend on your current health concerns, your destination, and your level of physical activity, but it doesn't hurt to check with your doctor before you head out, especially if you're on any kind of medication. If it makes sense in your situation, ask your doctor to jot down the key points of your medical history, including your medications (listed by brand, generic, and scientific names), allergies, serious health conditions, and blood type. (Note that you may be charged a small fee for this.)

It's essential to see your doctor or a travel medicine specialist if you're travelling to countries where certain vaccinations or anti-malarial drugs are needed (see below). Be sure to assess these requirements three months before you leave (six to eight weeks at an absolute minimum) because some vaccinations take that long to become effective, and others may need to be specially ordered.

Of course, if you have a serious health condition you should wear some kind of MedicAlert jewellery to let emergency personnel know what they may be dealing with if you're unable to tell them yourself. It can help to include a card in your purse or wallet that contains additional details.

Don't forget dental care. Toothaches or loose fillings can quickly turn a vacation into a nightmare, especially if your trip takes you to a place where dental treatment isn't up to the standards you're used to at home. A check-up and cleaning a few weeks before you leave is a smart idea.

Also check that your travel medical insurance is adequate (see "Medical Insurance" in Chapter 2, Insurance: Cover Yourself!) to ensure that you're completely covered for the destinations you're going to and any health concerns that you may have.

You may also want to prepare a medical kit (see the checklists at the end of the book for an essential Travel Medical Kit) that you can carry. It's a good idea to keep this with you, rather than putting it into checked luggage. However, with current security regulations prohibiting sharp items such as scissors, and restricting liquids and gels, either make sure that the kit doesn't include those items (put them in checked luggage) or put the entire kit into checked luggage, keeping out any medication that you may need on the plane. Those who need to carry medical necessities such as syringes and needles (diabetics, for example) should travel with a certificate from their doctor.

After the trip, if you feel ill—even if you think you just have the flu—within a few weeks of your return, go for a medical check-up to make sure that you haven't picked up something more serious (let the medical staff know that you've been away). International travel has brought new diseases to North America and Europe, along with some diseases that we thought had been almost eradicated. That's why it's so important to ensure your vaccinations are up to date, and to let medical personnel know where you've been travelling.

An Ounce of Prevention

Diseases such as malaria and typhoid are often associated with developing countries. However, you can run into them, and a variety of bugs like them, that will produce serious or (rarely) fatal illnesses in developed areas, too. It's essential to check which vaccinations and/or medications you'll need for your trip well before you plan to leave (see the list of resources at the end of this section).

Be aware that if you're travelling to regions such as Africa and Asia, the vaccinations can be expensive, especially if you go to a specialized travel medicine clinic. If you're on a budget, check with your doctor or public health agency to find out if there's a less expensive way to get the vaccinations and medications that you need.

You may already have the yellow-covered booklet that's known as an "International Certificate of Vaccination." If not, you should be able to find one through your local pharmacist/chemist or public health agency. It has space to list all the vaccinations you've received, and is an excellent record, not just for yourself and your doctor, but also for use when entering countries that require specific vaccinations (such as yellow fever). It's a good idea to photocopy this book so that you'll have a record of the vaccinations even if you lose the book. Make two photocopies, so that you can take one with you and leave one at home.

The most likely vaccinations that you'll need will be against Hepatitis A and Hepatitis B. You've probably already had a tetanus vaccination. If not, consider getting one, or a booster if necessary, before you leave. Other possible vaccinations, depending on your destination, include typhoid, yellow fever, cholera, meningitis, polio, and rabies. Some vaccinations can leave you feeling tired, a little sore at the point of injection, or perhaps as if you have a mild case of the flu. It's a good idea to ask about potential side effects beforehand, and to schedule the vaccinations when you have time to take it easy for a day or so if necessary.

Unfortunately there's no vaccination against the many forms of malaria that are found around the world. Instead, some type of "prophylaxis," or preventive medication, is prescribed, often an antibiotic. You'll generally need to start the medication before you leave, take it while you're travelling, and continue taking it for a period of time after you return. It's essential that you take the right medication for the malaria strain that's found where you'll be (not all medications work against all strains), so be sure you're receiving well-qualified medical advice, and take all medication exactly as directed. Keep in mind that the medication's only a preventive measure. You also need to combine it with common-sense insect-bite prevention (see "Insects and Other Critters" below).

To help you determine potential health risks at your destination, check out these resources:

- Foreign & Commonwealth Office (United Kingdom): www.fco.gov.uk
- International Association for Medical Assistance to Travellers: www.iamat.org
- Public Health Agency of Canada: www.phac-aspc.gc.ca
- Travel Health (United Kingdom): www.travelhealth.co.uk
- Travel Health Online: www.tripprep.com
- US Centers for Disease Control: www.cdc.gov
- US Department of State Overseas Citizens Services: http://travel.state.gov
- World Health Organization: www.who.int

Medication: A Movable Pharmacy

With many countries very concerned about illegal substances such as drugs, it's essential that any medication you take with you be clearly and legally labelled. It's also essential that the name on the medication prescription label matches the name on your ticket letter for letter. First, create a list of all your medications: include the name of the drug, the doctor who prescribed it and the clinic phone number, and the pharmacy or chemist and its phone number. Carry this list with you in your purse or carry-on luggage.

Since the last thing you want to do while on vacation is run out of medication (including over-the-counter remedies that may not be available where you're travelling), be sure to stock up before you leave. To avoid taking large bottles of pills with you, purchase travel or smaller sizes so that you can keep the items in their original packaging. For prescription medication that comes in large quantities, your local pharmacy or chemist may be able to print out an official label for a smaller container. It's also a good idea to check the regulations about taking medications into the countries in which you're travelling, as some may prohibit certain drugs.

If you do find that you need medication while you're away, don't do what one of our clients did: he bought penicillin on the black market when his wife became ill. Not only did the insurance company not cover the US$200 cost, he also took a huge legal and health risk. Many medications sold outside of reputable pharmacies aren't at all what they appear to be. They could be expired or even counterfeit. At best, they won't work; at worst, they'll make you even sicker than you were in the first place, and insurance companies may not cover the cost of dealing with the medical side effects of black market medication.

Lagging Behind: Jet Lag Solutions

Jet lag is your body's reaction to the confusion caused by travelling—usually flying—across several time zones. For most people, it shows up as sleepiness at the wrong time of day or insomnia, and a feeling of being in a bit of a fog.

It's also not unusual to feel disoriented, to have trouble concentrating (making map-reading and driving a challenge!), or to have stomach or digestive troubles. While these symptoms generally only last about one to three days, you don't want to spend the first part of your vacation dealing with them. Instead, try to minimize the jet lag right from the beginning of your trip.

If it's practical, try to start adjusting to the new time zone before you leave. Stay up a little later or go to a bed a little earlier for a few nights before your departure (depending, of course, on whether you're flying into a time zone behind or ahead of you) and adjust your wake-up time accordingly.

It's also useful (but, from personal experience, sometimes impossible, to be honest) to get a good night's sleep the night before you travel, so that you start your trip well rested and relaxed. Even if you can't get a decent night's sleep, at least make sure that you minimize your stress levels by allowing yourself plenty of time to get to the airport, for example.

When you're planning a long journey, such as North America to Australia, it can help to stop over for a night somewhere. It gives you a break from the plane, and it can ease the jet lag at your final destination. If you can sleep on a plane, it may help to plan your departure time so that you're flying overnight. But if sleeping's a challenge on board, your best option may be to fly so that you arrive at your destination in the late afternoon or evening. You'll have a couple of hours to get settled in, and then you should be able to sleep for an entire night.

Give yourself a break on the first day. If you have important meetings or a long drive on the schedule, plan them for the second day or later.

I always set my watch to my destination's time as soon as I get onto the plane. The cabin crew often tell you in their introductory remarks what time it is at your destination, or you can ask them. Getting used to the new time zone as soon as possible is a great way to reduce jet lag. If you need to grab some shut-eye, do. Sleep deprivation is a huge source of stress for most people, so trying to stay awake can be as bad as the jet lag itself. For daytime arrivals, wake yourself up with enough time to perhaps have a snack or breakfast and walk around the plane before you land to get yourself into "daylight" mode.

Bring a small pillow, blanket, sleep mask, and earplugs with you in your carry-on bag if you can, as many airlines no longer supply these amenities on board. To ensure that you're disturbed as little as possible in flight, do up your seat belt over your blanket so that it's visible to the flight attendants, and let them know as well that you don't want to be woken up for a meal. Keep in mind, however, that if there's turbulence or an emergency, they'll likely wake you for your own safety.

You may want to talk to your doctor about light sedatives, too, if you know that sleeping on the plane is going to be an issue. Try them at home first, so that you'll know what their effect is on you before the trip. The same goes for digestive or tummy issues—ask about stool softeners or motion sickness remedies, just in case.

To stay awake at your destination until it's an appropriate time to sleep, get out in the daylight. Go for a walk, take some deep breaths of fresh air, and resist the urge to sleep. If you absolutely have to have a nap (especially if you need to be alert to drive), set your alarm to wake you within about 20 minutes. You need to feel refreshed, so you don't want to let your body slip into a nighttime sleep pattern. Trust me, you'll wake up feeling groggy and grumpy if you nap too long. (See Chapter 11, All in the Family: Travelling with Kids, for tips for children.)

Healthy Flight Plans

The following tips will help to minimize jet lag, and will also work to keep you comfortable and as healthy as possible during flights:

- Dress for comfort, and in layers if possible. Planes can often be quite warm when you're on the ground, and cool up above—or vice versa, depending on the season. Clothing shouldn't restrict circulation, and shoes should definitely be comfy, because your feet can swell during the flight. If you have circulation issues (including being on contraceptive medication), talk to your doctor about circulation-boosting socks or pantyhose. It may also be advisable not to remove your shoes during the flight in case you can't fit your feet back into them afterwards.

- Avoid caffeine and alcohol, both of which can make it difficult to readjust your sleep patterns, and can also lead to dehydration. Also avoid fizzy, carbonated drinks as the gases can make you feel uncomfortable. Instead, drink plenty of water or fruit juices.

- Consider eating before you board, or bringing your own food on board. A light meal is better than a heavier one. Be sure to bring snacks, too, in case you get hungry between food services on board. There's nothing worse than being trapped in your seat with hunger pangs and no way to ease them. Some experts also recommend choosing lots of proteins for breakfast and lunch when you arrive, and lots of carbohydrates for dinner (the carbohydrates can help make you feel sleepy). If you have food allergies, such as nut sensitivities, be sure to notify your airline about them before you fly. Many airlines now serve pretzels or chips instead of nuts because of this, but it's always possible that a passenger will bring some on board. Carry your anti-allergy medication (such as an EpiPen) with you, along with MedicAlert information and a prescription for the medication.

- The air inside planes is notoriously dry so it's essential to stay well hydrated (which has the added benefit of reducing fatigue). If you can (check carry-on luggage restrictions), bring a small tube or bottle of moisturizer with you for your face and hands. Also consider wearing your glasses rather than contact lenses if your eyes are sensitive. And try to drink one litre of water (34 fl oz) for every two hours that you are in-flight to keep yourself hydrated.

- Some people find take-offs and landings quite painful on the ears and sinuses. Talk to your doctor before your trip about whether antihistamines or a nasal decongestant spray would help (these may also help if you end up flying when you have a cold). Chewing a piece of gum, sucking a hard candy, or sipping water can ease the pressure because they involve swallowing, which can help to equalize the pressure in your ears (which is why some airlines give out hard candies before take-off and landing). Some people have found that a product called EarPlanes, available at many pharmacies or airports, can also help. Note that babies in particular can be quite vulnerable to ear pain on planes. Experts recommend feeding them or giving them a pacifier to help ease their discomfort.

- Use your fan. If your seat partner is coughing up a lung, turn on the fan above your seat and point it towards you and to the side of your sick neighbour—and don't get into a deep conversation with them. If someone beside you is really sick, ask the flight attendant if you can switch to another seat.

- Wash your hands every chance you get and try to keep them away from your face. Everything you touch on that airplane has been touched by at least 50 people before you, so carry hand sanitizer if possible, or antibacterial wipes.

- Bring your own amenities. Unless they're wrapped in plastic, avoid such onboard provisions as blankets, pillows, and headsets. Who knows what ailments the last person who used them had?

Deep Vein Thrombosis: DVT Danger

The dangers of deep vein thrombosis have become more recognized in the past several years. Basically, this is a condition in which a blood clot forms—often in the legs—due to restricted circulation. If the clot moves to the lungs or the heart, it can be fatal. It's certainly very rare, but do speak to your doctor about it, especially if you are at risk due to medical conditions (including being overweight), being a smoker, or medications that you're taking (including contraceptive medication).

While you're travelling, whether you're flying or simply limited in your ability to move around on a bus or a train, make sure that you take frequent breaks to stand up and walk as much as you can. If you can't stand up, at least do some exercises while seated. Wiggle your toes and tense and relax your muscles (especially in your legs) regularly to keep the blood flowing. Avoid crossing your legs, or sitting in exactly the same position for too long, which can also restrict circulation, and be sure to stay well hydrated.

Water, Water, Everywhere...

...and not a drop to drink! With apologies to Samuel Coleridge ("The Rime of the Ancient Mariner"), it's not only salt water that's the problem for travellers—it's all water. Even if you're travelling in an area where the water is considered safe to drink, its mineral and chemical content could be different enough from your water at home to cause some stomach upset, even if you're only travelling short distances.

Of course, in many areas of the world, the water isn't safe to drink at all. That means you not only need to choose bottled water to drink (always check that the plastic cap is properly sealed before you take that first sip), but you should also exercise caution around anything that could have been made from or washed in local, unsafe water. Salads are common culprits, as are ice cubes. If in doubt—don't. Remember, too, to brush your teeth with bottled water, and to avoid swallowing water while you shower.

If you can't find bottled water, you can try bottled soft drinks and juices, or you can boil or chemically treat the water with special tablets or filtering equipment. Research the option that makes the most sense for where you're travelling.

Food for Thought

My motto for safe eating is: Boil It, Cook It, Peel It, or Forget It! Keep this in mind at all times and you won't go wrong. Typical villains when it comes to various types of food poisoning include mayonnaise- or cream-based recipes, buffet foods (do you know how long they've been sitting out there?), shellfish, street vendor food, and anything raw.

The other villain may actually be you, or more specifically, your personal hygiene habits. It's essential to wash or clean your hands thoroughly before eating, especially when you're travelling. Similarly, if you're suspicious of the cutlery, don't use it. Depending on where you're travelling, you may wish to bring a small set of your own travel cutlery, or plastic cutlery, just in case.

Dealing with food allergies or sensitivities—or just plain dislikes—can be a challenge, especially if you're speaking a foreign language. If you have any concerns, make sure that you learn a few key words or phrases to let restaurant staff know what the problem may be. You may even want to write the phrases down and carry them with you, in case your pronunciation isn't as good as it could be. (For language translation cards, you can check out the products available through www.selectwisely.com.)

Given the often flexible and spontaneous nature of travel, you may find that meals aren't scheduled or available when you'd normally eat, especially if you're relying on planes, trains, or buses. It's a great idea to pack an assortment of snacks when you travel. Avoid carrying fresh fruit or veggies, of course, because they'll be confiscated when you cross national borders, but pre-packaged snacks such as meal replacement or granola bars can go a long way to staving off hunger pangs when you either can't obtain food right away or the food's simply not to your taste.

Part of the attraction of travelling is experiencing the local culture and that, of course, includes local food specialties. Consider trying these by all means, but do your homework before you leave so that you'll know what the dishes likely contain and how they're prepared. This should give you a good indication of whether or not they're a good idea.

And don't forget that many of us tend to overindulge when we're on vacation. Not only can that lead to digestive upsets, but it can also show up after we return home in the form of extra weight that we have to lose. It's best to opt for "everything in moderation."

Motion Sickness: Oh, Those Waves

Even those with iron-cast stomachs may find themselves feeling queasy if they get stuck at the back of a bus that's lurching around corners, or on a small boat that's bobbing around on the waves. Cruise ships generally have excellent stabilizers to minimize the ocean's effects and will also route around rough seas to ensure their passengers' comfort, but if you're particularly sensitive to motion, you may want to plan ahead.

Talk to your doctor or pharmacist before you leave about the best remedy for you, depending on your health, where (and how) you're travelling, and how sensitive to motion you are. Also try to figure out what makes you feel better: focusing on the horizon (and avoiding reading and sewing, for example), eating crackers, sipping flat ginger ale, lying down, or standing up.

Oops! Common Maladies

Traveller's tummy is probably the most common illness you'll encounter while away. Experts generally advise waiting it out if you can, rather than immediately trying to stop the symptoms, because diarrhea and vomiting are the body's natural defences against bugs. It's essential to maintain your fluid levels, however, to prevent dehydration, especially for children, seniors, or anyone with a compromised immune system, so try to drink lots of bottled water and watered-down fruit juices.

If it's more than just a straightforward tummy upset, however, seek medical help: if you see blood, for example, or you're running a high fever, or if it just won't stop on its own after several days. You may also need to resort to medication if you have a travel day ahead, when frequent bathroom breaks just aren't possible.

Clean and treat cuts and scrapes with an antiseptic cream immediately, especially if you're in a tropical area: warm, moist conditions can create infections very quickly. Similarly, take an anti-itch gel or spray with you to treat insect bites, because scratching them can lead to infection. A product such as calamine lotion can also be helpful if you're vulnerable to heat rashes, as can antihistamine medication.

Dehydration and too much sun can make even the healthiest person feel quite ill. Be sure to maintain your fluid intake (it's not the most appealing health check, but the colour of your urine can provide a good warning: if it's a light straw colour, you're generally well hydrated; if it's dark, you're not) and avoid alcohol if you suspect you're dehydrated, because it can cause you to lose fluids.

"Medic!" Finding Medical Assistance

You have a number of options for finding medical assistance when you're travelling, depending upon the urgency of the situation. First, check with your medical insurance coverage. Phone the number that's always provided with the insurance policy to find out what they recommend in your area, and whether they have contact information for reputable local medical care providers. You can also check with your hotel or tour operator, because they often maintain a list of English-speaking medical personnel whom they can contact for you.

Travel Best Bet!
One colleague of mine was at the pyramids in Egypt when she recognized the signs of a bladder infection. As soon as she returned to her hotel she asked the reception staff if they had a doctor on call—and sure enough, they did. He was trained to Western standards, spoke English, and was able to immediately provide the antibiotics needed to solve the problem quickly and effectively.

If you're staying with friends and family, check with them. Their family doctor or medical clinic may be willing to see you. Credit card emergency-assistance phone numbers (especially with gold or platinum cards) or your nation's local embassies or consulates may also be able to help. You can also contact the International Association for Medical Assistance to Travellers (www.iamat.org). Membership in this organization—which educates travellers about health risks and maintains contacts with Western-trained doctors who speak English—is free, although they do appreciate donations.

Whatever medical assistance you obtain while you're away, try to get a written record of it. If that's not possible, take down as many pertinent notes as you can so that you remember which treatments or medications you may have been given. When you return home, you should check in with your family doctor to make sure that whatever the medical problem was it's now well and truly solved.

It can sometimes be difficult to assess when you need medical assistance. Certainly seek medical advice immediately if you develop a high fever. Packing a small digital thermometer can come in handy to help you judge whether you're ill enough to seek medical attention right away. Otherwise, use your judgment. It can be worth a few hours out of your vacation to receive the treatment or medication (or even just reassurance) that will make the rest of the trip much happier and healthier.

Insects and Other Critters

Do all that you can to avoid mosquitoes and other biting insects that can carry various nasty diseases, from malaria to the West Nile virus. It's good to check whether the mosquitoes or insects that transmit disease are more prevalent at certain times of day, such as during the evening. Whenever they're present, wear long-sleeved shirts and pants, and regularly apply repellents containing DEET. DEET has been linked with health concerns, particularly for children, but many experts feel that its risks are less than those posed by potential exposure to diseases such as malaria. Talk to your doctor or travel medicine expert before you leave to find out the latest information and tips. Also try wearing light colours and avoid using scented soap, scented lotions, and perfume. At night, sleep under a treated bed net or behind screened windows, and check that there aren't any holes in the nets or screens.

It sounds like it should be common sense to avoid touching local animals, but when you're sitting at lunch and a stray puppy wanders by to beg, or a monkey perches on the fence behind you, it's tempting to give in to the cuteness factor. Keep in mind that even the cutest animals can carry pests such as fleas and ticks, and may even be suffering from serious diseases such as rabies. If you're bitten, seek medical attention immediately to assess whether a rabies shot is needed, and also to prevent infection in the wound. Research the prevalence of rabies in your destination country before you go.

Handy Health Hints

If you wear glasses, you already know that you'll lose or damage them when it's most inconvenient. Take along an old pair as a spare, just in case you run into a problem while you're away, and especially if you require eyeglasses for essential tasks such as driving. Some countries actually require you to keep a spare pair of glasses in your vehicle if you need them for driving. Also bring a travel repair kit with a small screwdriver and extra screws.

It can be really difficult to feel clean and refreshed while you're on the road, especially if the water quality's questionable. Antibacterial or antiseptic wipes and hand lotions (such as gels that don't require water) will have you feeling cleaner in a jiffy, and are small enough to tuck into a purse or a pocket. Putting a day's supply of wipes into a resealable bag helps to keep space issues under control, and even a toothbrush and toothpaste in another resealable bag can help—you can use bottled water to rinse.

Wherever you are, but particularly in high-sun areas, apply your sunscreen regularly. If you're going on a beach vacation, take it easy on the sun lounger for the first day or so. Overdoing it can cause you pain and anguish for the rest of your trip. Remember that the sun is strong at alpine ski resorts, too, and it's even possible to get sunburnt on overcast days. You should also check your medications: some can cause you to become more sensitive to sunlight, which means that you'll be much more vulnerable to sunburns.

Keeping your shoes on when you're outside is always a good plan. It helps you to avoid insect bites, and provides some protection against garbage (such as nails or pieces of glass) that may be hidden in sand. It can also be advisable to wear some form of water-appropriate shoes when snorkelling or wading, as some species of sea life can inflict a nasty sting if they're stepped on.

Be aware that swimming in some areas of the world can expose you to something called schistosomiasis. This nasty disease is caused by a parasite that can lead to damage to your liver, kidneys, and other organs. It's definitely one to be avoided! Even if you see the local people swimming, it doesn't mean that it's safe for you to do so. Always check with a reliable guidebook or local expert first.

You can reduce the chances of being involved in motor vehicle accidents by respecting local rules of the road, giving way to other vehicles (even if they're in the "wrong"), observing speed limits, wearing seat belts/helmets, using car and booster seats, and avoiding night driving or driving when you're tired (especially if you're jet-lagged). (See Chapter 8, On the Road: Renting a Vehicle, for more driving tips.)

And if you're indulging in romance while you're on vacation, always practise safe sex. Use your common sense and use a condom.

Flying While Pregnant

Whether or not you travel when you're pregnant should be a decision that's reached between you and your doctor or your team of health-care professionals. Air travel can be the major issue here, with many airlines requiring a signed doctor's letter authorizing you to fly if you're within 7 to 28 days of your due date. Certainly, if yours is a high-risk pregnancy, you may be advised not to travel at all, whether or not the journey involves flying.

Each airline has its own rules, but there are two that are common across the board: one, you need a doctor's note certifying that it's safe for you to travel; and two, any airline reserves the right to deny boarding to a pregnant woman if it believes her safety or its liability is at risk (even if you have a doctor's note!). The stage of pregnancy at which these rules kick in may vary, depending on the airline.

Check with your travel insurance provider to find out whether your cancellation and medical coverage applies during pregnancy, and if so, whether it's valid for your entire pregnancy. Some policies restrict claims payouts after a certain point in a pregnancy.

Once you've determined that it's safe and healthy for you to travel, and you're covered by your insurance, there are a few things that you can do to make it easier. For example, carry your insurance policies, doctor's phone number, and recent medical records with you, just in case you need them while you're on the road. Many of my friends and colleagues have said that it was difficult to travel in the first trimester, because of the fatigue factor, and in the third trimester, because of the extra weight and discomfort. That leaves the second trimester as the time when they felt best equipped to travel, but of course, that's going to be an individual decision, too.

Make sure you drink plenty of water while you're travelling, especially if you're flying, and take a break to move around at least hourly, even if it means stopping the car and extending your journey time if you're driving. If you're drinking lots of water you'll probably need frequent rest stops anyway. Request an aisle seat where applicable. It will be more comfortable to get in and out of, and you won't disturb anyone on your many bathroom trips. Train travel may be a better option than flying if you're pregnant. It's easier to move around in a train coach than on a plane. A small inflatable pillow can help to ease a sore lower back, whichever way you're travelling. In cars and planes, make sure that the seatbelt isn't resting on your stomach; it should be wrapped around your hips so that it doesn't injure your unborn child if there's a sudden stop or bump.

Food can be a huge issue for pregnant women. If you know that you have a sensitive stomach, bring your own tried-and-true snack foods and make sure that you're eating regularly. Also bring doctor-approved medications or remedies for queasy stomachs, even if yours has been settled for a while.

Travel Best Bet!
I travelled several times during each of my two pregnancies. I found that my second trimester was the easiest time to travel. I was already over the morning sickness, had lots of energy, and wasn't so big that it was uncomfortable or cumbersome to travel. If you have a healthy pregnancy, I would absolutely recommend a getaway before life becomes busy with a newborn!

CLAIRE'S BEST BETS FOR STAYING HEALTHY

- Find out which vaccinations or medications you need for your destination at least three months ahead of your trip, and then make sure that you get them.

- Talk to your doctor well ahead of time if you have any health concerns, including pregnancy.

- Bring clearly labelled medication containers for prescription medication, and bring the prescription itself, in case the medication is lost or stolen and needs to be replaced.

- Watch what you eat and drink while you're travelling: if it can't be boiled, cooked, or peeled, don't eat it. Stick to bottled water and refuse all drinks containing ice cubes.

- If you feel ill when you return from a trip, seek medical advice immediately and let the doctor know where you've been travelling.

Chapter 5

Staying Safe

"Is It Safe?"

That's one of the questions that travel advisers are increasingly hearing from travellers. It's an understandable concern: no one wants to invest their hard-earned money and time in a vacation that jeopardizes their safety. However, the reality is that if you use as much common sense when you're travelling as you do in your home city, you'll likely be just fine. Unfortunately, it's all too easy to leave your common sense behind when you take off on vacation.

Of course, travel does bring a few concerns of its own. You may not be familiar with the areas to avoid at your destination, you may have to deal with natural disasters that you're not used to, and you may encounter scam artists or thieves who specifically target travellers. To minimize these risks while still enjoying your vacation, focus on three main areas: understanding your destination, recognizing scams, and avoiding setting yourself up as a target.

The Official Word: Government Travel Advisories

The Canadian, British, and US governments all maintain a careful watch over what's happening in the rest of the world, making their websites an excellent resource if you have questions about destinations. No matter what your nationality, it's useful to compare what all three countries have to say about various travel destinations:

- Canada: www.voyage.gc.ca
- United Kingdom: www.fco.gov.uk
- United States: http://travel.state.gov

Assess the information on these sites carefully. They come in two general types: country reports (which may describe a country's political, geographic, and demographic characteristics, including safety considerations) and various levels of notices, advisories, or warnings (which are stronger suggestions to beware of specific activities or areas, or to avoid travelling to an area or country completely).

If any government is advising against travelling to a particular place that you'd still like to visit, talk to your travel agent or check the Internet discussion boards at such trustworthy sites as Lonely Planet (www.lonelyplanet.com) to find out what other travellers are saying. But remember that nothing is worth more than your health and safety. Don't take unnecessary risks.

Also keep in mind that if your government has issued a travel advisory or warning about a destination and you choose to book a trip there despite the official advice, a trip cancellation insurance policy will most probably not cover you if the political situation forces you to cancel the trip. (See Chapter 2, Insurance: Cover Yourself! for more on this.)

Know Before You Go

Familiarizing yourself with your destination during the planning process can help you prepare for any risks that you may encounter. For example, June 1 to November 30 is considered to be hurricane season on the US East Coast and Gulf of Mexico Coast, and through Mexico, the Caribbean, and Central America. Make sure that—whatever the risks—your trip cancellation insurance policy covers them.

Other sources of helpful information include friends and family who may have travelled recently to the destination. Guidebooks can also be helpful, but check out when they were printed as they're often written six months to a year before the date of publication.

Also find out if there are restrictions on your behaviour while in the country. The most common is restrictions on what you can photograph. In some countries, photographing transportation facilities such as airports or train stations, government offices, or military facilities can land you in big trouble.

Traveller Beware: Common Travel Traps

As long as there have been travellers, there have been people taking advantage of them. That's why it's essential to know the company you're dealing with when you're booking or paying for travel, especially when you're using the Internet. Arm yourself with two rules and you won't go wrong: first, buyer beware; and second, if it sounds too good to be true, it probably is! Now add two more rules: always read all the fine print; and, if in doubt, ask questions. If still in doubt—don't!

If you're dealing with a local company, check with your area's Better Business Bureau (or equivalent) to see if there are any complaints on record about the business, and whether the complaints were resolved successfully. You can also check with your municipality or county to see if a local business has a proper licence to operate.

The following travel traps include the most common that you should be watching for.

NON-INCLUSIVE PRICING

Airlines tend to be the major culprits on this one, advertising their "low, low fares" to various destinations and only adding in (often considerable) taxes and surcharges once you book. Airport improvement fees are part of this, sometimes being included as part of the airline ticket and sometimes being paid right at the airport. I totally appreciate the frustration people feel with the pricing of travel. In fact, I strongly believe that advertised pricing should include all taxes and have pushed for this to happen while sitting on travel industry advisory boards. Unfortunately, for as long as we have been in business (and well before), travel has been priced this way, with only the base fare advertised and taxes and surcharges additional. As confusing and sometimes downright misleading as this is, it will take government intervention to mandate this across the board before anyone starts to state the total price including those nasty additional fees. So, as always, read the fine print carefully to ensure that you understand exactly what you're paying for.

This warning also applies to "all-inclusive" vacations, which are often not as inclusive as you may think. You'll often pay extra for alcoholic drinks, for example, but some resorts or cruises take it even further, charging you for using certain restaurants or even for soft drinks.

> **TBB** *Travel Best Bet!*
> *A colleague recently checked out a company that was offering an all-inclusive package for a historical tour of France. It sounded great, until a close reading of the fine print revealed that the package did not include airfare to France, admission to museums, or lunches and dinners. It would have been more ethical for this company to advertise that it was "semi-inclusive."*

MEMBERSHIP-BASED TRAVEL CLUBS

You need to check these out carefully to ensure that what you're getting for the price of membership is really worthwhile. For example, a few years ago there were several variations on "last-minute travel" clubs that offered access to last-minute travel deals if you paid a membership fee. Today, there are plenty of ways to obtain last-minute travel deals for free, including through travel agents and trusted Internet sites.

TOUGH SALESPEOPLE

Timeshare salespeople have a well-deserved reputation for the "hard sell," sometimes making potential customers feel quite intimidated about the process. If you're attending a presentation (as is offered at many timeshare-oriented resorts and properties) and you feel uncomfortable or even "trapped" in the room, you need to get up and leave straight away. Then lodge a complaint, either with the resort's management or with the parent company. **NEVER** sign anything on the spot. Take any documentation home to be reviewed by your lawyer, no matter how great you think the deal may be or how much the salesperson tells you that you will save by signing immediately!

Another option is the newest trend in "purchasing" vacation properties: fractional ownership. While a timeshare only gives you the right to a certain amount of time per year at a resort, fractional ownership gives you a portion (upwards of 10 to 25 percent) of the property itself, which may equate to, say, three months a year. It may cost more than a timeshare, but you have the power to sell, bequeath, and otherwise control the property—and the salespeople can be lower pressure.

Common red flags when dealing with salespeople include being told that you have to decide on the spot, or that you should make your cheque out to an individual (rather than a company). If you sense a red flag, just walk away. Quickly.

DON'T CALL ME...

You get a phone call or a certificate in the mail bringing great news—you've "won" a free or deeply discounted vacation. Don't believe it. Usually you'll end up paying a lot in extra fees that the original salesperson or certificate didn't mention. Make sure you know all the details, and never send money to a company that calls you first. Even if you actually get to go on the trip, you'll likely find that it's very poor value for what you've paid, even if you haven't paid very much.

ACCESS TO TRAVEL AGENT "PERKS"

Beware of anyone offering to give you access to special discounts, or other perks that they tell you are given to travel agents, in return for a fee. First of all, you can't become a qualified travel agent just by paying any kind of fee—it takes significant training. Second, many of those "perks," such as reduced fares or special trips, aren't designed for consumer travel at all—they're tailored for the kind of volume or group bookings that travel agents handle.

Also, keep in mind that because of the number of people fraudulently claiming to be "travel agents" these days, travel agents cannot just show a business card to get the special "agent" discounts. Proper IATA-issued travel agent photo ID cards are required and checked by airlines, hotels, cruise lines, car rental agents, and anyone else offering such discounts.

OUT OF BUSINESS

In the past few years, several airlines and tour companies have gone out of business without warning, often leaving consumers wondering what to do with an airline ticket or vacation confirmation that's now worthless. You can protect yourself first and foremost by booking with a reputable airline or agency, but even that may not be enough.

Protect yourself further by using a credit card to book. Most credit card providers allow you to request removal of charges for items that you don't receive. That way, even if the airline or tour company doesn't refund you, you can still have the credit card provider reverse the charge. Check with your credit card provider about possible time limits on these claims.

Also make yourself aware of any industry or governmental programs to protect consumers. Some Canadian provinces, for example, have a travel industry assurance program that will reimburse consumers if an airline or travel company goes under financially. (See "Travel Agents: A Traveller's Best Friend" in Chapter 1, Planning for Paradise.)

BUMPS ON THE INFORMATION SUPERHIGHWAY

While the Internet can be a source of excellent information and deals, it also harbours many people who are looking for your money or, even worse, your financial identity. If you're searching for travel deals on the Internet, stick with companies that are well known and completely trustworthy. Otherwise you could end up providing your credit card number or personal details (such as birthdate, social insurance/social security number, home address, and phone number) to someone who not only has no intention of providing you with the travel, but who will then use the information fraudulently, potentially even stealing your financial identity. Always, always know who you're dealing with, and never provide any kind of information to someone you don't trust implicitly.

Even when you do trust the provider, stay alert. Crooks have been known to hijack legitimate websites or to create very similar-looking websites to obtain credit card numbers illegally. If they're asking you to use PayPal to pay for your travel, that's a sure sign that something's not right. Watch for red flags, and if something feels "off," look for an alternative.

Safety First: En Route

Whether you're at an airport, train station, tourist attraction, hotel, or vehicle rental agency, there are some basic things you should do (or avoid doing) to keep yourself and your possessions safe.

PAPER CHASE

Neck pouches or security belts are the safest ways to keep your passport, other travel documents, and money out of the hands of pickpockets. It's also a good idea to divide up your cash and put it in different places so that if one stash is stolen, you'll still have the rest. That goes for credit cards, too.

If you trust your hotel, and it has a safe, this can be a good option for storing valuables such as extra cash that you don't want to carry around with you. I always recommend keeping key documents such as your passport on your person, however. Your passport is the most important travel document you own, so treat it like the valuable commodity that it is.

If you're carrying traveller's cheques, make sure you keep their serial numbers in a different place from the cheques themselves, and keep an extra copy of the serial numbers at home. If you can't prove what the serial numbers were, you'll have a much harder time replacing the cheques. Keep the contact information for the lost/stolen cheques call centre with the serial numbers, just in case.

While you're at it, keep photocopies of your passport and other essential documents in a different place from the originals. You'll be amazed at how much the copies will help if the originals are lost or stolen. This goes for credit cards, too. Keep the phone number for lost/stolen cards, and other emergency numbers, in a separate location from the cards themselves.

LUGGAGE LOTTO

It's incredibly easy to lose track of your luggage. A few moments of inattention, especially in a crowded airport terminal, and it's gone for good. To start with, make sure your luggage is labelled, inside and out, with your name. Don't, however, use your home address on the label. A work or post office box address is safer in case the luggage is stolen.

You may also consider using a luggage alarm that will sound if the luggage is moved suddenly and will alert you to a bag that's being snatched. Don't rely solely on alarms, though. Make it difficult for the bag to be broken into or stolen: lock it with a lock or a lockable security strap (see "Securing Luggage: Can I Use a Lock?" in Chapter 3, Ready... Set... Prepare! for more details on using locks). If you're waiting somewhere, keep your luggage attached to you in some way. Wrap the straps around your arm or leg, for example, and keep items such as handbags and camera cases around your body, not next to you.

Travel Best Bet!

A well-travelled friend of mine recently toured parts of Italy and ended up on the same train as a young Australian tourist whose daypack, containing a digital camera and US$500 in traveller's cheques, had been stolen just moments before. She kept that in mind when, a few days later, she was waiting at another train station. She hooked the straps of her and her companion's luggage together so that every piece of luggage was connected to something else, and she wrapped one strap around her arm as she sat down. Even if someone had tried to grab a bag, they wouldn't have been able to take it very far, as it was weighed down with the rest of the luggage and a person!

Whether you're at an airport or anywhere else, never agree to carry luggage or packages for someone you don't know, even if they look like the sweetest possible person. You're responsible for whatever's in your possession. Period. When you're going through security line-ups, especially at airports, make sure you keep your eyes on your bags. Thieves have been known to walk off with items from the conveyor belts, especially smaller items.

Don't keep valuables in the outside pockets of luggage, especially backpacks or daypacks. And don't stow these items under the seat in front of you in such a way that the pockets are within reach of the seat's occupant.

Just as you should at home, be careful to stow your luggage in the trunk, not the back seat, when you're in a vehicle. Keep valuables out of sight so they won't provide an opportunity for a snatch-and-grab.

Keep jackets and coats with you if you can; if you have to hang them up, make sure you take any valuables out of the pockets.

PERSONAL PRIORITIES

Consider registering with your nearest consulate or embassy when you're travelling, especially if you're in a less stable area (you can often register by phone or online). At the very least carry the office's phone number and address with you in case you need it.

It's a good idea to check in regularly with family or friends at home so they know where you are in relation to your itinerary. It's very easy and inexpensive to do this via a free e-mail account in Internet cafés, but keep hygiene in mind in these very public places. Be sure to wash your hands thoroughly after using a keyboard at an Internet café and avoid touching your eyes while you're actually using the keyboard.

Even though roaming and long distance charges can make cellphones expensive to use outside of your local calling area, nothing beats them in a crisis. It's possible that cellphone networks may go down or be restricted following a major catastrophe, but it's still worth carrying one that will work under normal circumstances at your destination. Check with your provider to find out about service areas. If your destination isn't included, consider buying or renting a cellphone that will work (some vehicle rental agencies, for example, will also rent cellphones for the duration of your rental). Remember to take a charger with you, including a car charger if you plan to rent a vehicle.

Always stay alert when you're travelling. It's important to know where you are and who's around you. Avoid using a headset in public places because you won't be able to hear important noises such as someone approaching from behind or a car horn. Hotel staff can often let you know which areas you should avoid, especially after dark.

 Travel Best Bet!
One colleague, who was walking through downtown Amman, Jordan, on her own, found the winding streets too complicated to follow on the map. Despite not wanting to reveal herself as a tourist, she pulled out her map twice to check where she was. Both times, a kind passerby immediately stopped to ask if she needed directions or help. It's good to be careful, but be open, too.

Travel experts often recommend that you shouldn't "look like a tourist," and I agree—to a point. Avoiding the fanny-pack, white-sneaker tourist uniform is always a good idea and by all means do your best to blend in with the local populace, but be realistic—in many areas, you're going to look like a tourist, no matter what you do.

By the same token, it's not a good idea to stand on a street corner looking lost and holding your map wide open. You're still likely to need your map, no matter how carefully you study it before you leave your hotel room or your cruise cabin, but try folding it into a manageable, more subtle, reference so that only the area you need is visible. If you get lost, find a bench or stand with your back to a wall while you're looking at your map, so that if someone approaches you, you'll see them coming.

I don't necessarily recommend travelling on your own—groups can certainly be safer—but sometimes it feels good to strike out independently. If you do, just make sure that someone knows where you're going and when you'll be back; and make sure that you're back when you said you would be. That's when a couple of cellphones shared between the group can come in very handy. When you're out on your own, if you sense at any time that you're getting into an area you don't like, trust your intuition. Turn around and retrace your steps.

When you're making calls, using the Internet, or using credit/debit cards, always shield your actions so that people can't see or hear any personal information that you may be entering or saying. Remember that identity thieves may even use binoculars.

Take taxis (make sure they're legal taxis, which are marked and licensed), especially at night. Be sure to take a business card from your hotel with you to show to the taxi driver on the way home, in case he or she doesn't understand where you want to go. If you're driving, consider valet parking to avoid parking garages, especially if the garage isn't part of the hotel building. In historic areas of Europe, you may find that the garage is a block or so away from the hotel itself.

Remember, it's all about common sense. If in doubt, don't.

Pickpocket Prevention

The tips above will go a long way to keeping your valuables safe, but pickpockets deserve a special mention, simply because they're so prevalent in many areas of the world where people love to travel. And they're very, very good at what they do. A cluster of adorable small children approach you, giggle a little, and then disappear—along with the wallet that one of them has lifted out of your back pocket. It happens all the time.

To avoid having it happen to you, pay attention to where you keep valuables such as wallets and purses. Wallets should never be in back pockets. Keep them in front pockets, in zippered pockets, in money belts, and anywhere that's more difficult for a pickpocket to access. Purses shouldn't be worn over the shoulder. If you have to carry one, put the strap over your head so it can't be easily snatched away from you.

Some travellers use a fake wallet. They may fill it with an old (and not use-able) credit card, a little bit of cash, and one piece of identification that's easily replaceable. If a thief demands their wallet, that's the one they give, and it's also the one they keep in their back pocket. If it's stolen, they lose very little.

Help! What If I'm Robbed?

If you do have the misfortune to be robbed or mugged while you're travelling, keep in mind that most thieves don't intend to be violent. Stay calm, give them what they ask for, and most important, don't resist. If the situation is relatively calm, you can ask them to leave you your identification and just take the cash and cards, but don't push your luck in a volatile situation. A fake wallet can be handy in this situation, but if the thief isn't satisfied with that, remember that no amount of money or hassle to replace your documentation is worth being injured or worse.

Whether you were robbed in person or simply had some belongings stolen, cancel your credit and debit cards immediately and report the theft to the local police. Make sure that they give you a written report because you'll need it to make an insurance claim. If you need medical assistance, call the emergency number on your travel medical insurance policy to check in with the insurance company before seeking treatment. If it's an emergency, however, simply contact them as soon as humanly possible.

After all that, you have to start the process of replacing traveller's cheques and identification, and putting your vacation back on track. If you need assistance, don't hesitate to contact your nearest consulate or embassy. Do your best not to let the experience taint your opinion of your vacation destination or its residents, or to affect your enjoyment of your trip.

Girls Get Away Safely

While women travel safely all the time on their own, it's important for female travellers to use their common sense. The last thing that you want to do is put yourself in an unsafe situation. Research can make all the difference, especially if you're travelling overseas to an area with a culture that has different gender expectations. Understanding the local culture is essential. It also shows respect.

When you're travelling to a foreign country, follow the local traditions and customs as much as possible. Try to blend in if you can, perhaps by dressing and behaving conservatively. Observing how the women around you behave and are dressed is always a good guide in conservative areas. Also make sure that you have a few basics in the local language, including "no" and "help."

Be wary about meeting men on your own, even if it's a business situation, and especially if you're in a country where you know the attitudes toward women are different from those at home. Wherever you are, avoid advertising to people that you're travelling or staying on your own.

Some women who are travelling in conservative areas will wear a wedding ring whether or not they're married to help avoid unwanted advances or comments. If you do find yourself in an uncomfortable situation, move away from it: sit or stand near other women, or near couples.

Again, use your common sense. Try to avoid travelling after dark, and keep a fully charged cellphone and whistle with you. Never, ever leave your drink unattended or accept a drink from someone you don't know or have just met. The risk of the drink being doctored with a sedative drug is just too great.

For great tips and a wonderful sense of community for women travellers, check out www.journeywoman.com.

Checking In: Staying Safe in a Hotel

Whether you're male or female, hotel room safety tips apply equally. When you're booking hotels, ask about whether they use electronic key cards for rooms, whether the rooms have peepholes in the doors, and whether the front desk is staffed 24/7. All can add a measure of safety. Consider that upper-floor rooms can be less vulnerable to break-ins via balconies than lower floors, but may be less safe in case of fire.

When you get into your room, make a point of reading the fire escape and safety information. Always know what your primary and secondary fire escape routes are. Depending on the hotel that you're in, don't rely on their smoke detectors. Use your own portable detector to give you an early warning. If you do hear a fire alarm, don't ignore it. Walk, don't run, to your nearest safe exit. Keeping your purse or wallet, your clothes, and a small flashlight next to the bed can help you exit quickly but don't put your safety at risk to find your valuables. Remember what you learned during school fire drills and just get out quickly and safely.

If you're concerned about room safety, ask for a staff member to carry your luggage to your room and have them enter the room first. Check the room out, including the bathroom, while the staff member is still there to make sure everything is okay. When you leave the room for any time, leave the radio or TV on and put out the "do not disturb" sign to make it appear that you're there. Always push the door and try the handle when the door closes behind you as you leave to make absolutely certain that it's closed and locked.

Be discreet about your room number. If you're paying for meals in the restaurant, or collecting your key from the front desk, ensure that you're not overheard when you give your room number. If you're really concerned, write it down rather than say it out loud.

Be alert. If someone knocks on your door unexpectedly and says that they're a hotel employee, ask to see identification (through the peephole) or call the hotel operator in order to verify the employee's name and purpose.

Staying Safe When It's Not Safe

Your travels may occasionally take you to developing or politically unstable areas, or to an area that becomes unexpectedly unsafe, perhaps because of rioting or a natural disaster. If this happens, there are actions that you need to take to ensure your safety.

First, make sure that you've registered with your government's nearest consulate or embassy (you may be able to do this by phone or over the Internet, to make things easier). If you haven't already registered, do so right away. If the government organizes an evacuation—as they have done in the past from places such as Lebanon, for example—they need to know that you're in the country, and how to reach you, in order to help you.

Second, do your best to find out what's happening and where the safest place is for you, but don't put yourself at greater risk to do this. For example, avoid political demonstrations, rallies, and other crowd situations. Crowds can be volatile, and the group mood can deteriorate very quickly. Even more important, if the local authorities move against the crowd, you could end up being classified as a protestor—or even worse, as a foreign agent. It sounds like something from a spy movie, but it has been known to happen.

Third, try to remain as calm and patient as possible. This is a difficult situation, but it's not going to get any easier—for anyone, including your travel companions—if you panic. Try to assess the situation, stay where you are if it's safe, and wait out the immediate crisis.

Prepare Like a Boy Scout: Pack These Essentials

Carrying a fully-charged cellphone, and emergency numbers for people such as friends, family, insurance company, consulate, and airline, will help you be prepared for just about anything. It's also a good idea to tuck a few items into your luggage for "just in case" scenarios. Include a small battery-operated alarm clock and radio, a pocket flashlight, some emergency cash, a couple of snacks such as granola bars, and pen and paper. A portable smoke detector can also add a margin of safety, duct tape comes in handy for everything from hemming pants to sealing your hotel room door against smoke, and a rubber doorstop can help hold your hotel room door against intrusion when you're in the room.

CLAIRE'S BEST BETS FOR STAYING SAFE

- Understand travel traps to avoid getting caught in them.
- Know your destination, and its risks, so that you can avoid getting yourself into unsafe situations.
- Remain alert at all times, and keep a close eye on personal belongings.
- Know a few words in the local language, and carry small denominations of cash to make it less likely that you'll be taken advantage of by people trying to scam tourists (e.g., taxi drivers, store clerks, tour guides).
- Avoid wearing expensive clothing or jewellery, or carrying expensive luggage.
- Lock car doors and hotel room doors at all times.
- In a crisis, stay calm.

Chapter 6
Air Travel: Flying High

Booking Your Flight

Quite frankly, finding the best airfare can be a challenge—even for someone like me, who has been in the travel industry for years. The airlines' rules about which type of ticket you fly on, and when, can be confusing at best and chaotic at worst. It helps to do your research thoroughly, of course, or ask a travel agent to find and book the most appropriate flight for your needs. But however you choose to book, make sure you understand all the limitations, extra fees, and other rules that come with your ticket.

 Travel Best Bet!
I cannot count the number of times I've heard about people missing flights because they read their flight schedule incorrectly. Most travel documents use the 24-hour clock versus "a.m." or "p.m." as this typically helps prevent confusion. However, people do still get confused. The most common error I see is travellers showing up on the wrong day for flights leaving just after midnight. For example, if you're set to depart on September 7 at 0025, you must check in late on September 6. I've seen many people make the mistake of showing up late on September 7 to find their flight had left almost 24 hours before they arrived!

As soon as you get your travel documents—whether they're traditional paper tickets or e-tickets—it's essential to review all the details carefully: dates, names, flights... everything. If something needs to be changed it's much easier—and potentially much cheaper—to do it right away. **DO NOT** wait until the day before you leave to do this. It may be too late by then to correct an error. Remember, too, that the name on your ticket **MUST** be your legal name—the same one that's on identification such as your passport—otherwise you could be denied boarding. Even if you have always gone by a different name (e.g., a middle name or a shortened version of your legal name) and that name appears on some of your important identification (such as credit cards), you cannot book an airline ticket in that name. You must use your full name—no initials—as it appears on your passport or other government-issued identification that you're travelling with. This applies to children as well as to adults.

MAXIMIZING FREQUENT FLYER PROGRAMS

There are plenty of ways to collect credits on frequent flyer programs, from airline plans to mileage-accumulating credit cards to programs such as Air Miles. With all the options currently available, you could theoretically accumulate miles on earth-bound items such as grocery or gas purchases and use them to fly high to your next vacation destination. There are, however, a few things you should know.

First, it's important to go with a reliable plan—with an airline that's not likely to disappear, for example. This is absolutely imperative if you want to save your miles for a big trip: you need some assurance that the airline will still be around when it's time to take that trip. It's equally important to understand all the details. With some plans, for example, points will expire if the account isn't kept active by further accumulations of points or redemptions.

To maximize your mileage, try "double-dipping." For example, if you purchase an air ticket using a mileage-accumulating credit card you'll get the frequent flyer miles from the airline (if you qualify), plus points from the credit card. Watch for specials from the programs, too: for example, bonuses for flying at certain times or on certain routes, bonuses for using specific partners, and redemption discounts.

When you're ready to redeem your points, pay attention to flight prices. If you can get an inexpensive flight to your destination, you may be better off paying for the flight and saving your points for when you can't get a cheap flight. For example, if you want to fly to a destination that's only served by one airline, your flight will likely be more expensive than if you're flying to one served by several airlines that are competing for your business. Using the points on the more expensive flight gives you maximum value.

 Also, stay flexible when you're redeeming your points. Book as early as possible and be willing to change your travel dates by a few days, in case your first choice of travel date is sold out. (Midweek flights can sometimes be easier to find, for instance.) For the latest on all the travel rewards programs, I visit www.rewardscanada.ca. You may also find www.awardplanner.com, www.frequentflyerbonuses.com, and www.webflyer.com useful for finding frequent flyer programs and booking reward seats.

FINDING LOW FARES

Okay, all you bargain hunters out there, you're waiting for those great last-minute deals, aren't you? It's true that airlines always try to fly with full passenger loads, which used to mean that you might get lucky with a last-minute deal as they tried to fill seats. But here's the bad news: that happens far less frequently now, as airlines have trimmed their budgets, and therefore their schedules, as much as possible. These days the lowest fares are usually available when the plane is least full. As the plane fills up, the remaining seats become increasingly expensive. Think of it as the law of supply and demand, acted out on a plane-by-plane basis.

My advice is to book as early as you possibly can. A month in advance is essential, and even more is better. Although specific fares and requirements (having to stay over a Saturday night, for example) vary widely between airlines, I can give you some tips that will usually help you find the lowest prices. For instance, round-trip fares will almost always work out to be cheaper than one-way fares. Also, mid-week flights tend to be the least expensive; and Mondays, Fridays, and weekends tend to be more expensive. (Notice the emphasis on "tend to be" here—there are always exceptions to the rule, especially if the airline is trying to boost passenger numbers on a certain route.) If you're flying at peak times, you must understand that the most popular flights will be the most expensive and the most difficult to find. For example, flights the day before any major holiday will likely be booked up quickly, and will be more expensive. The same goes for the weekends prior to and after the holiday. If you can, travel on off-peak days or on the holidays themselves.

Travel Best Bet!
A colleague who recently wanted to fly into Paris, France, and out of London, England, compared one-way prices between Toronto, Ontario, and Europe. Using one-way fares would have cost her $2,500. By flying into Paris and out of London on the same airline, however, and using a low-cost airline or taking the train between the two European capital cities, her transportation costs were cut to $1,500.

FLYING STANDBY: NOT SO MUCH

Airlines used to offer many opportunities to fly standby or on a "space available" basis. These very inexpensive tickets were often the only way to travel for young adults and students. Business travellers also picked up on the standby option, using it to add flexibility to their schedules. These days, however, standby tickets are very difficult to come by for most airlines, for a couple of reasons. First, airlines are paying much more attention to fuel costs than they used to, so they're trying to encourage passengers to show up for their expected flights so that fuel calculations can be more accurate. And they found that passengers were using standby options to get around more expensive change fees. The bottom line? You'll likely only be offered a standby option if you've been bumped from an earlier flight or if you've missed your flight.

If you show up early at the airport and try to get on a flight that leaves prior to yours, the airline may allow you a standby option. However, some fares don't allow this, so check your restrictions before you try it.

BEREAVEMENT FARES

It's always stressful to travel because someone close to you is very ill or has passed away, and the high costs of last-minute flights can make it even more stressful. Most airlines offer some type of compassionate or bereavement policy to immediate family members (including grandparents and grandchildren) that either provides a discount or waives certain ticket restrictions such as ticket change fees, or both. There may be limits, however (some airlines restrict bereavement fares to international flights, for example).

Call the airline directly to find out what they can do for you. Expect to show proof of either illness or death. A death certificate or doctor's letter is the usual standard, but even the contact information for the funeral home or hospital involved may be enough. If you can't show proof, or there's not enough time to get the paperwork, ask about their policies for reimbursement after travel, when you will have the paperwork.

FLYING SOLO: BOOKING CHILDREN TO FLY ALONE

If your children will be taking a flight alone, especially if they're 12 years old or under, you need to book their flight well ahead of the date of travel. Airlines are increasingly requiring that solo kids fly only on direct or non-stop flights; that is, they can't travel alone on flights that stop en route or require plane changes. If you're a parent trying to get your child across the country this can seem really frustrating, but the rationale is actually quite sound. If the itinerary is disrupted for weather or mechanical issues, for example, your child may end up having to overnight alone somewhere. This can be scary for them and is an overwhelming responsibility for the airline.

Also expect to be charged an additional fee for kids travelling alone. This is to offset the cost of airline personnel staying with the children prior to take-off, and escorting them to and from the plane. (See also "Flying Solo: Children Travelling Alone" in Chapter 11, All in the Family: Travelling with Kids.)

GETTING A GOOD SEAT

If you can, check the seating plan when you book your flight to find out where the best seats are in your ticket class, based on the aircraft that you'll be flying in. Look for exit rows and seats towards the front of the plane. It can be worth the extra fee that some airlines charge to book the seat you want, especially if you're travelling with children. Airlines do switch aircraft, however, and sometimes at the last minute, so it's best to think of this strategy as potentially helpful but not a guarantee.

When you're considering exit rows, always check first with the airline. Although the exit row seats usually have more legroom, on some aircraft they don't recline. These rows will, however, give you a chance to fly without children next to you as emergency procedures don't allow children to sit here. They require someone who has the strength and ability to deal with opening the aircraft's door in an emergency (which is why if you're unwell or physically injured, such as having a broken leg, you won't be placed in emergency exit rows).

If you and a companion are travelling on an aircraft that has three seats together in its rows, consider booking the seats on either end of the row (often a window and an aisle seat). You may get lucky and end up with an empty seat between you, because the middle seats are the least requested. If you do have someone between you, they'll likely welcome the opportunity to switch with one of you, allowing you to sit together.

When you check in, you can always ask if there are any better seats available. If you have a specific request—for example, to sit with a travelling companion—the staff may be able to accommodate it then, or at least transmit a message to the onboard crew to try to accommodate you. You can also ask to be seated next to an empty seat, but of course that seat may become occupied as people continue to check in for the flight.

When you board the aircraft, you can also ask the flight crew if it's possible for you to switch seats. Of course, you'll only be able to do this if the flight isn't full, or if another passenger agrees to the switch. If you're asked to switch seats with someone, consider agreeing. Although you won't always be rewarded, airlines occasionally provide bonuses such as upgrading you to business class. I've found www.seatguru.com to be an excellent source of detailed seating plans and onboard amenities for many different airlines and planes. It even notes the position of power ports and seats with limited recline.

AVOIDING FLIGHT DELAYS

Some flight delays are inevitable: there's absolutely nothing that you can do to avoid them. But you may be able to reduce your chances of encountering a delay, or at least to minimize its length. Non-stop flights offer the best strategy, because the fewer airports you're stopping at, the fewer chances you have to be delayed. Early morning flights can also help, because if there's a delay or cancellation, you'll have a better chance of having your flight be one of the first out, or rescheduling on a different flight the same day.

CONFIRMATIONS AND RECONFIRMATIONS

Confirm your flight details with your airline about 48 hours before your flight is scheduled to leave, and then reconfirm them just before you leave for the airport. This gives you the best chance of actually getting on the flight, and it lets you know if there are any last-minute changes. If you've made any special requests, such as vegetarian meals, double-check that they're still there. If you haven't already made your seat selection, you may be able to do it when confirming your flight details.

THE AGE OF TECHNOLOGY

Those of us who are used to booking a ticket and then waiting for a multi-part, red-carbon-copy ticket to arrive must accept that our glory days are fading fast. Increasingly, you'll be e-mailed an electronic ticket from your airline or your travel agent that you print off yourself. At first, it can be difficult to wrap your head around this: will the airline staff really accept this piece of paper that you've printed from your own computer? Yes, they will!

> **TBB** *Travel Best Bet!*
> *Whether your ticket is electronic or paper, check it for two pieces of information: the ticket number and the booking reference (sometimes known as the locator number). Write these two numbers down and keep them separate from your ticket. If the ticket is lost or stolen, having those numbers will make getting a replacement easier.*

It's not just tickets that have gone electronic: check-in procedures have, too. Many airlines now offer the opportunity to check in online through their websites up to 24 hours before the flight departure. You simply follow their on-screen prompts, including confirming your seat and how many pieces of luggage you have, and printing out your boarding pass. All you have to do once you get to the airport is find the airline's express baggage drop-off, present your ticket and your boarding pass, and hand over your luggage.

If you don't check in online you can use the express check-in kiosks that many airlines now offer at the airport. Instead of waiting in line to check in with a real person, you enter your details (such as frequent flyer number, booking reference, or credit card number) into the screen, print out your boarding pass while you wait, and then drop off any bags at the express drop-off.

At the Airport

I love heading to the airport. As I get closer, I get a rush seeing the planes take off and land. Whether I'm leaving on a trip, or just picking someone up, the feeling of excitement is always the same. But once I'm inside any airport, I rein in my excitement and put on my game face. That's because airports are notorious for theft, with thieves taking advantage of people who are heading off on vacation with their guard down and their possessions in small (easy to snatch) bags.

Airports are not immune to the risk of crime. So, as we discussed earlier, always keep an eye on your bags, your coats, and your valuables, such as wallets and purses (or better yet, attach them to you).

CHECKING IN

Remember two simple things and you won't go wrong. First, arrive early. Airports are very busy places these days, and line-ups for check-in, express baggage drop-off, security, and customs can be long. If the weather's not good or it's rush hour, give yourself extra time to get to the airport. A good rule of thumb in today's security climate is to arrive at the airport 90 minutes ahead of your flight for domestic flights and three hours for international flights, but always check with your airline to see what they recommend. Never, ever try to push their minimum boarding times. You could end up being denied boarding, which means you'll likely have to pay either for another ticket or for a change to your existing ticket.

Second, arrive with all the paperwork you need, including your ticket, boarding pass (if you've checked in online), and photo identification (you'll never go wrong with a passport, but for domestic flights, make sure that you at least have government-issued photo identification such as a driver's licence). Check that you have all of this before you leave the house. Anything else (toothbrushes, watches, for example) can be purchased at the airport or at your destination.

THINK SECURITY

It's imperative these days to think about security when you're packing your bags. Certain items can't be carried on aircraft at all—these include explosives such as fireworks or starter pistols, flammable liquids, "strike anywhere" wooden matches, poisons, and aerosols such as compressed gases. Other items such as scissors, knives, and sporting equipment with sharp points or edges (skates and darts, for instance) can't be put into carry-on luggage. Some of this is

common sense and has been in effect for some time, but I recommend checking with the airline and even with the Canadian Air Transport Security Authority
website (www.catsa.gc.ca) for the most up-to-date information possible. If you
do attempt to carry any prohibited items, they'll be confiscated. Period. For other
packing tips, see Chapter 3, Ready...Set...Prepare! and the checklists at the end
of the book.

Security technology is continually being upgraded. One of the latest innova-
tions is an X-ray machine that can see through your clothes. Not surprisingly,
one of the criticisms is that it's an invasion of privacy, but security officials are
using it because it can find objects hidden under clothing and not visible to
other scanning technology. If you're asked to go through this screening, keep in
mind that it uses very low X-rays and it doesn't store the images. Plus, security
officials are going to great lengths to assure people that no one's taking advantage of the machine. The operator will be the same sex as you, but won't actually
see you, only your image.

Because the rules change depending on the country, the airport, and the security risk, it's difficult to give specific guidelines here about going through security.
However, in any circumstance you should be prepared to be asked to remove
coats, jackets, and possibly shoes and belts so that they can be scanned on the
conveyor belt (slip-on shoes can be a huge help when flying in today's security
climate). If you set off the walk-through scanner's alarm, security personnel will
likely use a hand wand to scan for prohibited items. If you're asked to submit to a
"hand" pat-down, you should be taken to a separate area, and checked by a person
of the same sex as you.

Any electronics that you're carrying may also be submitted to a thorough
check. They're often checked for traces of explosives, and you may also be asked to
switch them on to prove that they're working.

I know that security measures are a major source of stress for passengers, but
you have to accept that they're here to stay, and unfortunately for good reason. Be
patient, even when the process seems especially frustrating. If you have a complaint, it's probably best to lodge it in writing after the fact, rather than to get angry
with security personnel at the time. If they're not happy with your attitude, they
have the power to stop you from boarding your aircraft. And, of course, never joke
about security when you're anywhere in the airport or on the plane: you could find
yourself behind bars very quickly, and I don't mean the kind that serve martinis!

OUCH! GETTING BUMPED

Airlines routinely overbook flights because they know that people will change
their plans at the last minute or miss their flights. The airlines want to fly with
a completely full aircraft and to do that they overbook the seats to give themselves a cushion for the no-shows. The problem is that sometimes the airlines

overestimate that cushion and suddenly they have too many passengers and not enough seats.

You can reduce the likelihood of being bumped by arriving early at the airport. Even better, use the online check-in option if your airline offers one. If you check in before you leave home you'll have a better chance of keeping your seat.

Depending on the airline, you may encounter different approaches to the overbooking problem. The check-in staff usually begin by asking for people to volunteer to take a later flight. If your schedule is flexible, it's worth considering because the reward is usually a credit towards future flights, or a voucher for cash. If it's a flight credit, be sure to check how restrictive its conditions are. If you think it's going to be difficult to use before it expires, opt for the "sure thing" of the cash. Restrictions to watch for include blackout dates, expiry dates, advance reservation requirements, and geographic limits (such as not being valid for international flights).

 Travel Best Bet!
A friend's sister was travelling from London, England, to Edmonton, Alberta with her four-year-old son. Even though she arrived at the airport in plenty of time, the airline announced that she, along with dozens of other passengers, had been bumped because a mechanical problem had forced them to replace the plane with one that was much smaller. Although the "bump" involved close to a 24-hour addition to her journey, she remained calm. She did, however, explain that she was travelling with a young child and that this was going to make the trip difficult for both of them. Was there anything that could be done? She and her son were offered extra frequent flyer miles, a healthy cash voucher, and business class seats on the other flight. She believes that she was given the only business class seats available because, while other passengers were yelling at the airline's staff, she was patient, making it clear that she understood that they were doing their best.

If you're bumped off your flight by the airline, it's considered an "involuntary" bumping. If this happens, the airline is required to pay you compensation, which varies depending on the length of your delay. However, the airline will often try to soften the blow a little more by offering other bonuses, too—extra frequent flyer points, or a seat upgrade, for example. If you're offered just the basic compensation, there's nothing wrong with asking (politely, of course), "Is that the best you can do?" Keep in mind that check-in employees are probably very hassled already, so remain as calm and pleasant as possible—but do still ask.

OOPS! I NEED TO CHANGE MY PLANS

It's always best if you can stick to your original travel itinerary, but sometimes you don't have a choice. If you need to make a change, call the airline or your travel agent right away. If that's not practical, show up at the airport as soon as you can and explain your situation. Either way, expect to pay the change fee associated with your ticket, along with any difference in cost between the flights that you booked and the ones that you're now taking. Your worst-case scenario may be flying on a ticket that doesn't allow any changes, especially at the last minute. Some tickets obtained through frequent flyer or mileage accumulation programs, for example, may come with provisions like this. In this case, you may find yourself shelling out for a whole new ticket. Ask airline staff to do their best to get you the best possible fare.

In some cases, if you can fly out earlier than your planned flight, and the airline has space available, it may be to everyone's advantage to get you out on that earlier flight. Offering to go standby for the earlier flight may get you home sooner, but check the fees. You obviously don't want to be charged a huge fee for flying standby.

If you think that there's a good chance that you'll have to change your flight plans, don't opt for the lowest fare when you book your ticket. They usually have the most restrictions and the highest fees when it comes to changes. Paying a little more up front can actually save you money down the road if you do end up changing your schedule.

OOPS! THE DOG ATE MY TICKET: DEALING WITH LOST TICKETS

If you've lost your ticket your first reaction may be to panic, but relax. It's less of an issue than it used to be. First, if you're flying on an electronic ticket and you still have access to the e-mail that sent you the ticket, simply open up the e-mail and reprint the ticket. If you don't have access to the e-mail, call the airline or your travel agent and ask them to re-send it. If there's no time for that, head to the check-in counter and provide your name, booking reference (if you have it), and a government-issued piece of identification. You should be able to obtain your boarding pass and another copy of your ticket there.

If you're flying on a traditional ticket, and it's lost or stolen prior to your arrival at the airport, call the airline or your travel agent and explain the situation. They may be able to forward a replacement ticket, or arrange for you to pick it up at the airport (although there may be a small fee for this). If you're at the airport already, head to the check-in counter and explain what's happened.

On the Flight

Whether you're flying for a couple of hours or a couple of days, there are ways to make the in-cabin time much more pleasant. Along with bringing fun things to read or do on the plane, here are a few places to start.

FLIGHT ETIQUETTE

As flying involves a large number of people in a small area, common courtesy from all passengers is very important for everyone's comfort. Be careful with your hand luggage to ensure that you don't bump people with it as you're entering or leaving the aircraft. Check behind you before you recline your seat, and avoid reclining it all the way if you think it's going to bother the passenger behind you. (Asking before you recline is a gesture that's often appreciated.) If someone is busy working or reading, it may be an indication that they don't want to talk, so avoid interrupting them.

If someone is bothering you, assess the situation. A simple request for them to stop the action (such as reclining their seat onto your knees) may be all that it takes. If it's not that easy, however, talk to one of the flight attendants (it's often best to leave your seat and have the discussion quietly and discreetly out of earshot of the individual in question, if possible). You can ask to be moved if there are seats available elsewhere, or you can ask for the cabin crew to deal with the situation.

AIRLINE FOOD: KNOW YOUR OPTIONS

The most important thing to know about food on airlines these days is that it may not exist. Airlines have been cutting food service to the bone, so to speak, in the last few years, in part to offset rising fuel costs and keep air travel affordable. On shorter flights—that is, typically less than four hours—forget it. You may get a small bag of pretzels and a beverage service if you're lucky. On longer flights, you might get a meal, but it could be a cold bun rather than a piping hot dinner. And on some flights, you'll get a meal only if you pay extra for it. Always check with your airline to find out ahead of time what, if any, meal service you can expect.

The airline terminal restaurants and shops have responded to this in ways that are actually good for you as a passenger. You can now carry on your own meal, whether it's sushi or a burger that you picked up in the terminal. If you have any allergies, keep them in mind when choosing food at the terminal. Bringing snacks from home is an even cheaper option if you're trying to stick to a budget. Remember, though, to check security regulations. You may not be able to carry bottles of liquids through security, and metal cutlery will be a definite no-no.

If you're lucky enough to be on a flight with food service, ask about the alternative food selections, which often include vegetarian, children's, kosher, low-salt, and other options. It's a bit of a gamble here, to be honest. Sometimes the alternative meals taste better than the regular ones because they're prepared in fewer quantities. They're also often passed out first, so you'll get to eat first (although your tray will be cleared at the same time as everyone else's). But on some airlines, the alternatives are a little bland. It's definitely worth experimenting, though, especially if you have restrictions on your diet. Be sure to request the alternative or "special" meals well ahead of time (many airlines have cut-offs for ordering special meals) and reconfirm the details when you call the airline to confirm or reconfirm your flights.

IN-FLIGHT ENTERTAINMENT

Technology is helping airlines to offer more, and better, in-flight entertainment than ever before. In fact, many airlines are switching from those awkward "head-always-in-the-way" overhead screens to individual TV screens in the backs of seats. At the same time, they're giving passengers individual control over what they want to watch, and providing a menu of options, from movies to news to sports. Other options that you may find include video games, satellite TV and radio, Internet and e-mail access, and phones. Just remember that the lower-cost airlines and the shorter flights are less likely to offer in-flight entertainment. And the systems do break down, so always bring your own entertainment, such as books, games, or DVD players, just in case.

Laptop computers and handheld communication devices can generally be used whenever the seatbelt sign is switched off, as long as their send/receive functions are switched OFF, to ensure that they won't interfere with aircraft operations. Game-playing devices can also be used in the flight, but must be put away during take-off and landing.

LONG-HAUL FLIGHTS

Trips that keep you cooped up on an aircraft for upwards of nine hours or more can be tough to take, even if the destination will be worth it. Here are few things that can make them more tolerable.

- Consider upgrading to business or first class, either by paying for it or by using frequent flyer points. The extra comfort can be worth it. Some airlines (British Airways, for example) also offer a small section of their economy seats that have slightly upgraded legroom or wider seats. This is also worth checking out.

- Look for a premium seat within the economy section of the aircraft. Some exit rows, for example, have more legroom than other rows, and some aircraft have an economy row that's just one or two seats wide where the seating configuration changes between business and economy. Check the aircraft seating plan when you book, and opt for the best seats possible. Keep in mind, though, that the airline reserves the right to switch aircraft without notice, so you could still end up in a less-than-ideal seat.

- Choose your seat based on your preference. A window seat might give you great views and a place to rest your head for sleep, but every time you want to stretch your legs or visit the restroom, you'll have to climb over or disturb the passengers next to you. An aisle seat sometimes means that you'll be bumped by passengers or crew walking in the aisles, but it does give you quick access to the facilities, and may make it easier for you to do your stretching exercises.

- Wear comfortable clothing in layers that you can add or remove as the aircraft cabin cools or heats up. Comfortable shoes are a particularly good idea, because feet can swell during the flight, making shoes feel tight.

- Bring plenty of items to read, watch, play, or do. Portable DVD players or electronic games can be especially useful to keep children occupied.

- Move around the aircraft as much as possible to reduce the risk of deep vein thrombosis (see Chapter 4, Staying Healthy), especially if you're at greater risk (if you smoke, for example, or have varicose veins, or are taking birth control medication). If it's difficult to walk around, at least do leg exercises in your seat: flex your feet and your calf muscles, and keep them as active as possible. Also consider circulation-boosting hose or socks. (Talk to your doctor before the flight.)

- Bring an eye mask and earplugs to help you sleep. Your own pillow and a shawl that will double as a blanket can also be helpful. Also talk to your doctor before the flight about options such as sleep aids or No-Jet-Lag pills.

FEARFUL FLYERS

While it's true that many more people are involved in serious automobile accidents than serious airplane accidents, that doesn't help you if you're afraid of flying—and since at least one out of six adults are, you're in good company. I recommend checking out the suggestions at www.fearoflyinghelp.com to put your fear into context and to give you some great techniques for handling it.

I'm always concerned that a fear of flying will prevent people from travelling or will interfere with their enjoyment of a well-deserved vacation. If the fear is severe, talk to your doctor about it. There may be medication or other techniques that you can use to ease your anxiety.

When you're on board, it's best to let the flight attendant know that you have a fear of flying. Flight crews understand the situation and can often do a lot to help you as long as they know ahead of time.

When you feel anxious, try to distract yourself with a good book, a funny movie, or anything that will work to take your mind off your fear. Breathing exercises can also help to reduce stress levels and prevent panic. Ask your doctor about how to do these correctly, but as a general rule, long, slow breaths are calming and short, shallow breaths can boost anxiety.

Understand and accept that the plane will make noises (when the wheels go up and down, for example) and may sway or bump in rough air. This is entirely normal. Keep telling yourself that if there's any reason to worry, the flight crew will let you know.

Anything that will increase your heart rate can contribute to a feeling of nervousness. This includes caffeine, so go easy on the coffee, cola, and tea. Although alcohol can have a calming effect on some people, I don't suggest it as a way to get through a flight. It dehydrates you and interferes with your ability to think clearly, which is not a good thing, and you may feel its effects more quickly or strongly than you would on the ground. Using alcohol to calm your nerves is also not advisable because ground or cabin crew can refuse to let you board, or stay on, the aircraft if you're obviously drunk.

Some people have found that snapping a rubber band against their wrist can help to stop the negative self-talk that winds them up into nervousness and panic. You may want to give this a try, but make sure that the band isn't at all tight.

Travel Best Bet!
NASA researchers are currently developing technology that will warn pilots several minutes beforehand that there are gusty winds ahead. This will give the pilots time to switch on the seat belt sign before they hit the turbulence and to contact air traffic control to request an altitude change or route diversion so that they can go around the rough air. This technology is already being tested on commercial aircraft.

Playing the Luggage Lotto: Lost and Damaged Bags

It's no fun at all when you're the last person standing at the baggage carousel and there are no more bags circling around and around. It's like an adult version of musical chairs, except this game has no winners. If you're at the beginning of your vacation, it's even worse: instead of heading off to the beach, the museums, or the ski hill, you're stuck at the airport terminal, filling in forms.

There is, however, some good news. First, the airlines are getting a lot better about lost and "misdirected" luggage. Statistically you stand a better chance of receiving your luggage in the right place at the right time than you used to. But that's cold comfort if you're one of the statistics that proves the exception to the rule. Here's how to minimize the chances of your luggage being lost, and maximize the chances of it being returned to you quickly.

- Choose non-stop flights wherever possible. The fewer the aircraft transfers, the fewer the opportunities for your luggage to go astray.

- Put identification on the outside of your bags, of course, but inside them, too, because luggage tags are vulnerable to being torn off. Avoid using your home address, as we discussed earlier. If you're carrying a cellphone, put that number on the tags. If not, use a number that has voicemail so that you can check messages.

- Take a photo of your bags and keep it in your carry-on bag. It's really difficult to remember what your bag looks like once it's no longer in front of you.

- Jot down a list of contents and keep that in your carry-on bag, too, just in case you need to claim them later on an insurance policy.

- Pack a change of clothes (or at least clean underwear) in your carry-on bag if you have space, along with toiletries that comply with security regulations at the time you travel.

- Don't put anything irreplaceable or valuable in your checked luggage. If it needs to come with you on the trip, carry it with you.

- Arrive at the airport in plenty of time to check your luggage so that it has time to make it to the plane.

- Check the tag that the airline check-in employee attaches to your luggage to make sure that it lists the right airport. (See www.world-airport-codes.com. It lists the three-letter code for almost any airport in the world that you're likely to land at.)

- If your luggage doesn't show up, report the loss immediately to your airline's baggage office. Some airports have a centralized baggage handling office, while others have individual offices for each airline,but the office is usually somewhere in or near the luggage carousel area of the airport. Have your baggage claim check handy. (It's usually stuck to your ticket voucher, boarding pass, or even your passport.)

- Fill out the airline's paperwork, giving as much detail as possible.

- Ask the airline what assistance they can provide while you're waiting for your luggage. In some cases, they'll offer toiletry kits, coupons to allow you to rent sports clothing (for example, if you're on a skiing vacation), or even small amounts of cash.

WHAT HAPPENS TO LOST LUGGAGE?

Your luggage will likely catch up to you within about 24 hours, but it can sometimes take longer. The airline is responsible for getting your luggage to you, within reason. If you're staying at a local resort, for example, they'll likely deliver to you via a courier. If you're departing on a cruise or tour, it could complicate matters, so be sure that you give the airline's baggage office a complete itinerary to make it as easy as possible for them to find you. Also let your hotel/cruise ship/tour operator know that you're expecting your bags to follow you.

Things can get more complicated if your bags are lost because you've been switched unexpectedly to another airline—due to inclement weather or mechanical problems, for example. In this case, you may need to deal with both airlines' baggage offices so that you can determine which one has responsibility for tracking your bags. A more complicated case such as this will require great patience on your part, and you should be prepared to give your luggage details several times to different people.

If you've cleared customs without your luggage, it's possible that the customs office will open your bags to check them, so don't be unduly alarmed if, when you're finally reunited with your bags, it appears that they've been searched. However, if anything's missing, report it immediately to the airline.

It's unlikely that your luggage will never reappear, but if the worst happens, you'll need to start the claim process, first with the airline and then with any other insurance coverage that you have.

WHAT ABOUT DAMAGED BAGS?

Whether baggage handling systems are automated or not, they're nightmarishly tough on luggage. Expect your lovely new suitcase to quickly acquire scuffs, dirt, and dings—all of which is another reason to buy decent quality suitcases made from tough materials, and to avoid expensive suitcases made from beautiful but easily damaged materials such as leather.

If the damage is serious—the suitcase has been ripped, or crushed, for example—go to the airline baggage office immediately. It's essential to do this before leaving the airport, so check your luggage over as soon as it arrives. Lodge a claim and fill out any required paperwork. If the airline accepts liability for the damage it may give you a voucher for a new suitcase, or for a local luggage repair shop (the latter option may be more common at your home airport since the repairs can take more than a few days to handle).

THE LIABILITY LIMIT

Under the terms of the fine print on your airline ticket, airlines are only responsible sible for reimbursing you up to certain limits for lost luggage that never resurfaces or bags that are damaged beyond repair. This is an international agreement known as the Warsaw Convention. Since the limit is usually based on weight, there can be a huge gap between what they'll pay (US$10 per pound) and what the contents or bags were actually worth. They also have a long list of exemptions that they won't cover (usually expensive items such as electronics, jewellery, eyeglasses, business items, and heirlooms such as old family photos). The exemptions are normally listed on the airline's website, so be sure to check it out carefully before you pack.

Once you've gone through the airline's claim procedure, check your household insurance and any baggage insurance policies that you have. They may help to cover the gap between the airline's liability limit and what the actual contents were worth. To avoid losing anything irreplaceable or very valuable, though, don't put it into your checked baggage.

CLAIRE'S BEST BETS FOR AIR TRAVEL

- Book early and try to be flexible with your travel plans to get the best fares and the best seats.

- Always, always check your flight details as soon as you get your ticket. Then check them one more time, just to be sure.

- To get better seats, ask at check-in and on the plane.

- Check in online if possible to save time in line-ups at the airport and to save your seat.

- Plan to arrive at the airport early (not just "on time") with your government-issued identification or passport and your ticket.

- If you get bumped, stay calm and polite, and ask about your compensation.

- Tag and identify your baggage carefully. If it gets lost or damaged, report it immediately to the airline's baggage office.

- Check in advance to find out about security issues, airline food, and other details that will affect your flight.

- If you're afraid of flying, speak to your doctor about measures to take that will help, and let flight attendants know, so that they can help.

Chapter 7
Cruises:
A Life on the Waves

Oh, for the Ocean Blue

Gilligan, eat your heart out! Today's cruise passengers are treated incredibly well. You can choose to cruise virtually anywhere in the world, from oceans to rivers, and on ships that range from freighters to floating luxury resorts complete with wave pools, ice rinks, climbing walls, and so much more. And cruising is a wonderful way to sample what the world has to offer. You can travel from place to place, seeing the highlights everywhere, yet you only have to unpack once and you never have to worry about navigating. When you factor in the hotel and transportation costs of other vacations, cruises can offer good value, too. Most of all, they can be low stress and high fun if you choose the one that suits your vacation style.

Here's what you need to know to get started on the cruise-ship lifestyle.

HOW DO I CHOOSE A CRUISE?

With such a vast selection of cruises out there, how do you know which one will be the best fit for you? Start by asking yourself some basic questions. The answers will help you narrow down your choices.

- *Where do I want to go?* If you have a firm destination in mind, such as Mexico or the Greek Islands, this is your logical start point.

- *Which waters do I want to cruise?* Cruise ships don't just sail the seas, they also head down rivers and canals, which can be a wonderful way to explore the interior of a country rather than its coastline.

- *How much time do I have?* Cruises range from three-day weekend getaways to year-round floating homes, so you can find a cruise to suit virtually any schedule. Some of the most popular choices include trips of 7, 10, and

14 days, but the destination may be the determining factor in the length of your trip. For example, if you're heading all the way from North America to Europe to cruise, you may not want to go with just a four-day option unless it's only one part of your trip. Otherwise you'll spend most of the cruise getting over jet lag and then packing up to leave.

- *What's my vacation priority?* Do you want to relax or enjoy the nightlife? Watch wildlife or shop 'til you drop? Go on eco-adventures or tour historic sites? Some ships are geared to older travellers, with more of an emphasis on history and culture, while others definitely set sail with "party" in mind. You don't want to end up on a ship with a crowd of passengers who are well out of your age or interest range. Some ships also offer specific "theme" cruises, ranging from music to casinos to archaeology. If you have a specific focus, these can be an excellent option.

- *Who's travelling with me?* Your vacation priority may not be the same as that of your travelling companions, especially if you span a significant age range. In this case, you may need to compromise and choose a cruise that will keep everyone fairly happy. This is one of the big advantages of a cruise: there's always plenty to do, both on board and on shore.

- *How much do I like other people?* This sounds like an odd question, but it's an important one. You can set sail with a handful of other people, with a few hundred, or with a few thousand. If you'd prefer a more intimate experience, you may prefer a smaller ship, which also has the advantage of being able to dock at a greater variety of ports than the larger ships. And if you really want to be adventurous, you can hop on board a freighter. They often take paying passengers and the choices available now are as vast as the oceans and waterways served by these ships. Expect rates to range from US$80 to US$140 per day for trips from 7 days to more than 100 days, and note that there is often an upper age limit, usually 79 or 80, but sometimes 75. There are exceptions, however, especially on shorter, coastal routes, and in those cases when more than 12 passengers are on board, when a medical doctor must be on board as well.

Travel Best Bet!

I've seen cruises offer groups of friends and families a wonderful vacation experience. In one case, five couples of varying ages travelled together. Some wanted to tour on shore, others wanted to shop, and others just wanted to relax. The cruise gave everyone the opportunity to do their own thing, and they had a great time comparing notes when they all met for dinner each evening.

WHAT ABOUT THE WAVES?

Many first-time cruise passengers are understandably concerned about being at sea, especially if they have a history of motion sickness. What about those waves? The good news is that modern cruise ships have high-tech and highly effective stabilizers, and the ship's captain keeps a watchful eye on the weather. If a storm is on the horizon the captain can—and will—adjust the ship's itinerary to miss the rough weather, even if it means missing a port call. However, you'll probably feel a little of the ship's motion and the general rule is that the smaller the ship, the more you'll feel. You'll feel less motion in the middle of the ship, and on the middle and lower decks. See "Avoiding Seasickness" on page 112 for more information about handling motion sickness.

HOW SAFE ARE CRUISE SHIPS?

The short answer is that they're very safe. They go through annual safety inspections for a start, their crews have substantial emergency training, and the ships are required to have lifeboat space and lifejackets for everyone on board, along with high-tech fire suppression systems and all kinds of other safety equipment. Problems do arise occasionally, though. For example, a large "rogue" wave caused some consternation for one ship not long ago, and there have been some isolated cases of fires breaking out or ships running aground. Overall, cruise ships—particularly those belonging to well known and trustworthy cruise lines—have very good safety records, but of course you need to be aware of emergency procedures, just as you would in a land-based hotel, for example.

In terms of your personal safety, you need to be as conscious of crime prevention on the ship as you would be on land. Think of the ship as a small city. You don't necessarily know who your neighbours are, so you need to exercise caution. Most people are on board either to earn a paycheque or to enjoy a vacation, but you do occasionally get someone whose intentions are less honourable. Protect yourself using common sense (especially at night). Be aware that strangers may not be who they say they are, and avoid setting yourself up as a target for crime: don't flash cash or gambling winnings around, leave the expensive jewellery at home, and pay attention to where you are and what you're doing.

Information Central: Researching Your Cruise

Cruise lines produce detailed guides about their destinations, ships, and itineraries, which you can request directly from the cruise line or obtain from a travel agency. The Internet is also an excellent source of background information, and can be a good place to start looking at what's available.

To get a sense of how the cruise lines and their ships measure up against each other you should surf on over to the Centers for Disease Control and Prevention (CDC) at www.cdc.gov. The CDC's Vessel Sanitation Program regularly inspects cruise ships for health issues such as food storage and preparation, general hygiene and cleanliness, and water quality. It then creates reports known as "green sheets" that score the ship's performance and describe any problems. A score of less than 85 out of 100 is considered "not satisfactory." The ships can also submit reports about the corrective action they've taken, so it's a good chance to see how seriously various cruise lines take the maintenance and cleanliness of their ships. (See also "Staying Healthy," later in this chapter.)

Although you can do a lot of research about cruising on your own, finding a travel agent with experience in booking cruises can be a serious advantage. They know the ships and the destinations well, they can offer helpful advice to match your vacation wishes with the right type of cruise experience, and they often have access to special packages, discounts, or upgrades. Also, travel agents can take care of other options, including pre- or post-cruise accommodation, transfers to and from the ship, and flights that work with your itinerary.

Travel agents can also assist with getting you to the ship on time, and with letting you know about any documents that you need for the trip, such as passports and—for some countries that you may be travelling to—visas. (See also "Paperwork: Beyond the Red Tape" in Chapter 1, Planning for Paradise.)

Cruising with Children

Many cruise lines these days are family friendly. Although I've heard some people say that they would never cruise with kids, I have to disagree. I wouldn't hesitate to take children if I found the right cruise, one that fit every family member's needs. Here are some pointers to help you find the right family cruise.

If your children are old enough to stay in their own room, book cabins across the hall from each other. You could book a more expensive outside cabin for the adults and a cheaper inside cabin for the kids. They'll love the freedom of their own room and bathroom; you'll love the rare taste of privacy, while still having the kids within reach.

To stay in touch with your kids, consider taking two-way radios. Remember to take extra batteries, and make sure the radios have both channel and code selection. On some larger ships you may run into someone using the same channel, in which case you can simply switch to a different channel or a combination of a different channel and code altogether. These radios aren't likely to cause any interference with the ship's equipment, but it's always a good idea to check with the cruise company beforehand.

Travel Best Bet!
I recommend that families booking two cabins (or two hotel rooms!) take a baby monitor that you can leave on at night. I find it helps Mom and Dad feel a whole lot better.

FAMILIES OF FIVE...OR MORE

I know from experience that finding a cruise line to accommodate a family of five can sometimes be tricky, especially when the kids are young and you all want to be in one cabin. But there are several cruise lines that can do it, including Carnival, Disney, Princess, and Royal Caribbean. The cabin configuration is typically two lower beds, two upper berths, and a rollaway. Most suites also accommodate five, and a typical configuration is two lower beds, a sofa bed that accommodates two, and a rollaway. Some ships also have connecting cabins for larger families.

These days most major cruise lines offer a youth program and have youth counsellors on board year-round to entertain children of all ages from morning to night. Youth programs start at different ages on different cruise lines, but they normally welcome kids of three years and older. Note that most will only accept kids who are potty trained, though some cruise lines have nurseries to take care of infants if you're looking for some adult sanity time.

Travel Best Bet!
If you plan on taking a toddler on a cruise and are worried about them falling out of the bed, take a collapsible bed rail. Safety 1st makes one that can fit into a large suitcase. I've travelled with it many times! Travel/rollaway cots are allowed in some staterooms, but not all, so if you're travelling with children who need a cot, check with your travel agent or cruise line about space issues. If a guest has mobility problems and can't reach an upper berth then a rollaway cot can be brought in, but only if the stateroom can accommodate it. Cruise ships don't have luggage restrictions, but of course airlines do, so factor that into the equipment you're carrying with you for children if you need to fly to your cruise departure port.

Save Us a Cabin! Booking Your Cruise

During much of the 1980s and 1990s there was excess capacity in the cruise industry, meaning that consumers could often find fantastic last-minute deals. However, in recent years cruising has taken off in popularity and even though cruise lines are constantly adding new ships and upgrading older ones, they're still barely keeping up with the demand. That's why you'll usually find the best deals if you book far ahead. The last-minute deals that you may see advertised will likely be for the cabins that are the least desirable: small, and "inside" the ship, without windows. Booking early also gives you the best selection of ships (many repeat cruisers have a favourite ship design), destinations, departure dates, and cabin categories and locations.

If you're looking for lower prices, consider sailing during the off-peak or shoulder season for your destination. For the Caribbean, for example, the spring and fall tend to be less expensive than the winter months; for Alaska, May and September are cheaper than the summer months; and for Europe, spring and fall offer lower prices than the summer. Check the weather, however, as it may be somewhat less than idyllic. June through November is hurricane season in the Caribbean, for example. That doesn't mean that you'll run into one, but it is possible that a storm could force your ship to change its schedule.

You can also ask about "repositioning" cruises. These are offered when the cruise lines need to move their ships between different areas of the world: for example, when they move ships that have been touring the Caribbean all winter across the Atlantic to start cruising the Mediterranean for the summer. You can also find some great repositioning deals when the ships transfer between southern itineraries in the winter and Alaska itineraries in the summer. May and September often find the ships doing short two-, three-, or four-day itineraries along the Pacific coastline, and the value can be excellent. Because there's usually more time spent at sea during these cruises, they're a little less popular than those that stick closer to shore, so the cruise lines offer good value in order to fill them up. They still offer port calls, sometimes in unique locations, and there are plenty of activities while the ship is at sea, so don't write them off as unsuitable without investigating what's on offer. You could also use all that extra time at sea to simply relax!

When you book your cruise, it's essential to add trip cancellation insurance and medical insurance if you're not covered on an annual plan. Imagine what would happen if weather cancelled your flights and you couldn't make it to the ship, or if you had to leave the ship early to handle a family emergency at home, or if you became ill while on board. A cruise can be a significant investment. Having insurance to cover your costs could mean that you'd be able to take your vacation later instead of missing out on it completely. (See Chapter 2, Insurance: Cover Yourself! for more information.)

A Berth with a View: Choosing Your Cabin

Choosing the right cabin on a cruise ship can be much more important than choosing the right hotel room. You may spend more time in your cabin than you would in a hotel room, and its position in the ship affects how much movement you feel, how much noise you hear, and how much of a view you'll have. Basically, the cabin's cost depends on its size, location, and window/balcony size. Accept that you'll only get what you pay for in this case.

If you don't plan on spending much time in your cabin, you may be just fine with an "inside" cabin that has no porthole or window. But there may be good reason to consider a cabin with a view. Many newer ships are incorporating balconies and large picture windows into a much larger portion of their outside cabins. If you're looking for a romantic cruise, for example, or if you prefer time on your own instead of with other passengers, a larger cabin with a private balcony may be worth the extra expense.

Make sure that you see the plan of the ship when you're choosing your cabin. The cabins in the middle of the ship and on a middle or lower deck usually experience the least of the ship's movement. Cabins at the front (bow) or the rear (stern) of the ship and on the upper decks pick up more of it. If you're looking for peace and quiet, avoid cabins near elevators, public areas, steward stations, laundry rooms, or stairs. The bow cabins can also be noisy because of wave noise and the anchor, whereas the stern cabins are often closer to the engine noise.

Also check that your travel agent requests the type of bed set-up that you need in your cabin: two separate twin beds, for example, or a queen-size bed. Keep in mind that some older ships have cabins with only upper and lower twin beds (like bunk beds), so be sure to ask!

Getting to the Ship

Unless you're lucky enough to live within a reasonable driving distance of a cruise terminal, you'll probably be flying to the terminal's nearest airport. The most important thing to remember is that planes get delayed, but ships tend to leave right on time (time and tide wait for no man, as they say) so build in some extra time between your flight's arrival and your ship's departure. You may need to clear customs at the airport, you need to get from the airport to the cruise terminal, you need to check in at the terminal for the cruise, and then you need to actually board the ship.

In some cases, the cruise lines offer fly-cruise or fly-stay-cruise packages, and these can be good value. They combine the flight with the cruise, sometimes with a hotel stay also added in for the night before the ship departs. The bonus here is that you can often tag your luggage right through from your home airport to the cruise ship. The ships pick up your luggage from your arrival airport, and take it to the ship for you—usually while one of their buses is taking you to their terminal.

The other bonus of booking all the travel arrangements using the cruise line's options is that if for some reason your flight is delayed, the ship will know about it, and in some cases the cruise line will even make arrangements to get you to the ship at the next port of call if necessary. Check with your travel agent to find out whether your cruise line offers this.

Whichever way you choose to travel to the cruise ship terminal—on your own or with the cruise line—consider arriving a day ahead of the ship's departure if possible. If your flight is seriously delayed, you'll still have plenty of time to make it to the ship.

I MISSED THE BOAT!

If by some unfortunate circumstance you don't make it to the ship on time, and the cruise line isn't responsible for getting you to the ship, all is not necessarily lost. If you can fly or drive to the next port of call before the ship is due to leave it, you may be able to join the ship then. Yes, it will add some expense to your vacation, but at least you won't lose your entire cruise. Before you do this, though, contact the cruise company to let them know what your situation is, and to ask their advice.

Setting Sail: On-Board Advice

A cruise ship is like a little community unto itself. It has its own mayor and police chief (the captain), plenty of "municipal" workers to keep everything running smoothly, and fun activities that make up an excellent leisure program. It also has a few personality quirks that you should be aware of. The following list includes the top issues that you'll likely encounter on a cruise. Forewarned is forearmed, after all.

SAFETY FIRST!

The very first thing that happens on board is the safety briefing. This is non-negotiable. You must attend, and yes, attendance will be taken. You'll be sought out if you don't attend and given the briefing anyway, so there's no point in not attending the first time around. You'll find your lifeboat assignment in your cabin. At the appointed time you need to make your way to the lifeboat and assemble there for a safety briefing. You'll learn about personal flotation devices (lifejackets or PFDs), how the lifeboats work, and what the emergency procedures will be. You could think of this as the equivalent of the flight attendant safety briefing at the beginning of every flight—except that this time, you'll have to pay attention.

DINING AROUND

Most of the larger, traditional cruise ships offer sit-down evening dining with a choice of an early or a late seating. Which one you request depends on your preference, but many people like the late seating because it gives them more time to enjoy being on shore during port calls. They don't need to think about returning to the ship for dinner early in the evening. People who enjoy the nightlife on board may prefer to start their evening with the early seating, and then move on to the show or the casino. Families with children may also prefer the early seating so that the kids can get to bed at a reasonable time.

You'll find that many of these ships use a variety of table sizes for dinner seating. Tables for two or four people may be in the minority, so you need to book well ahead to reserve them if you're travelling as a couple or a family and you don't want to mix too closely with your fellow travellers. Otherwise, consider going for a large table where you'll meet lots of people and will be somewhat shielded from the effect of travelling companions whose company you don't enjoy.

Newer ships, however, are moving away from formal dining like this to a more restaurant-like style where you can choose the time that you arrive and the location of your seat. Depending on your ship, you may even have a choice of restaurants. Cruise lines are definitely recognizing that many passengers don't like being locked into dining tables with people they don't know. It's undeniably a great way to make new friends, but it can be a bit of a problem if you find you're not compatible with the other diners. If you do end up with people you don't like, let the person in charge of the dining room know as you leave that first night, to see if other arrangements can be made. Remember to be polite and diplomatic about this. If you're really stuck, most cruise ships offer free room service.

WHAT SHOULD I WEAR?

The question of wardrobe is one of the first ones that passengers ask and it's a good one, but the answer depends entirely on the ship and the cruise that you've booked. Some ships are very upscale, where a long dress and tuxedo wouldn't be out of place for a formal dining night. Others, especially family-oriented ships, are very casual. Most fall into the middle ground, where it's bathing suits by the pool, shorts at lunch, sporty clothes for activities, and slightly dressier clothes for dinner. Your cruise ship's information will let you know what's appropriate. It's also a good idea to throw in a cozy sweater or raincoat, just in case, regardless of dress code.

SHORE EXCURSIONS

You'll likely have an opportunity to check out the selection of shore excursions offered by the cruise ship long before you set foot on board. They can be pricey, but they do have the advantage of being fully escorted, with reputable guides, stores that have proven themselves trustworthy, and a guarantee that you'll get back to the ship on time. In many cases, they can really help you make the most of your often short time on shore. It's a good idea to book excursions that you really want to go on before you leave. These days many of the popular excursions sell out before the ship even sets sail. Most cruise lines' websites will typically have a complete list of the excursions along with the option of booking them online or via a toll-free number.

There can be advantages to the "go-it-alone" approach, however. In many areas of the Caribbean, for example, you can hop off the ship, walk or grab a cab into town or to the attraction you want to visit, and enjoy a completely self-guided, self-propelled day. You choose how much you spend, where you eat, and how long you linger at each stop. If you prefer your independence to being guided around in a small (or sometimes large) group, this is a great option.

If you do choose the independent approach, bring along a guidebook or at the very least a map for your day's destination. A little research will let you know which direction you should be heading in, and will allow you to select the sights you want to see (and can see in the time you have available). You don't want to waste valuable shore time getting lost. Also, always, always double-check the ship's departure time as you leave, and plan on returning at least 45 minutes prior to that time. That way, if something goes wrong and you're delayed, you've given yourself a bit of a window.

You should note that all passengers returning to the ship have their cruise ID/room key scanned before boarding so the ship will known whether or not you've returned. However, the ship won't wait if you're not on board by departure time. It's the passenger's responsibility to be back on board the ship on time. If you miss the ship, it's your responsibility to contact the cruise line and to make your way to the next port of call to re-board the ship.

You can expect to find plenty of local taxis and guides waiting for you when you disembark for the day. To make sure that you don't get taken advantage of, you should know where you're going and how much a cab is likely to cost to get you there. The ship's crew may be able to advise you on this, but a guidebook to the area may be a better source of information. If you'd like the services of a cab driver or guide all day, negotiate a rate up front. If at any time you don't like the driver's or guide's behaviour, let them know right away and be prepared to walk away from them.

You may find that the value of shore excursions varies across different parts of the world. In southeast Asia, for example, having a local guide can help with language issues, and in Europe, the transportation that's included in the shore excursion can be good value when ports aren't close to the places you want to visit. Rome, for example, is quite a distance from the port that a large cruise ship will stop at. A little research and some discussions with your travel agent can give you an idea about which shore excursions would be better value.

POINT ME TO THE SHOPPING!

It didn't take cruise lines too long to work out that having hundreds, possibly thousands, of people on board provides a great retail opportunity. You'll likely find a selection of shops on board, along with cruise-line recommended shops in each port. The on-board shops can be expensive, so watch the prices, although the quality is likely quite good. The recommended retail outlets on shore may be more expensive than other on-shore outlets, but they generally offer reasonable prices for good-quality merchandise. If you have a problem with one of the recommended outlets, you'll be able to let the cruise line know by filling in the feedback forms on board the ship.

If you're looking for bargains, make sure that you do your research before you leave home. Many ports are known for certain items, such as jewellery. If you know what similar necklaces or bracelets would go for back home, you'll know whether or not they're worth buying when you're shopping on shore. You also need to remember to add on any taxes or duty that will be payable on your purchases on the way home. (See Chapter 13, Coming Home.)

 Travel Best Bet!
A friend was quite taken aback on her first Caribbean big-ship cruise. She showed up at the port lecture on board the ship, expecting to hear all about history and culture, but instead heard all about what she could buy in the stores on shore. The reality is that shopping is a huge draw for many cruise passengers, so cruise ships pay a lot of attention to it. If shopping's not your bag, though, the larger ships do offer plenty of other shore excursions, or you can look for a smaller cruise ship or a cruise with a specific interest, such as archaeology or nature.

STAYING HEALTHY

Although most cruise lines have stringent procedures in place to protect the safety of food and water, human error can happen. Use as much caution on board as you would when dining out anywhere else. Cream- and mayonnaise-based salads and desserts on buffets should be fresh. If you have any doubts, don't go there. Hamburgers and other meats should be fully cooked. If they're not, send them back to the kitchen.

Of course, if you have any allergies or food sensitivities, make sure that they're noted at the time you book, mention them again when you board, and then let your wait staff know, too. If you have any questions about the dishes or the ingredients, always ask.

Although the water on board is generally good quality, I prefer to go with bottled water—but that's a rule that I follow wherever and however I'm travelling. Bottled water can be a little easier on the stomach than other water because it contains fewer chemicals and its quality is a little more uniformly trustworthy.

One problem that has hit the cruise industry hard in recent years is that of the norovirus, often referred to as the Norwalk-like virus. This stomach bug isn't much fun, as it causes one to two days of digestive ailments such as diarrhea and stomach cramps. It's very contagious and easily spread between people in close quarters with each other. Well, you can see the potential in a confined place like a cruise ship, can't you?

The International Council of Cruise Lines (www.iccl.org) has responded with a recommendation that cruise passengers wash their hands thoroughly and often, especially before eating and drinking, and after touching items in public areas such as doorknobs. If you feel ill, head to your cabin and ask for the ship's doctor to visit you there, rather than walking through the ship and potentially spreading the ailment around. You may also want to check with your travel agent about what to do if you feel ill before you get on the ship. Cruise lines have recognized that making arrangements for sick passengers not to board can actually help everyone on the ship, so there may be something you can do to salvage your vacation cost, especially if you have cancellation insurance (which you would never travel without—right?).

AVOIDING SEASICKNESS

If you're prone to motion sickness, or you're uncomfortable in rough water, there are some remedies you can try. Your body is trying to adjust to the motion so give it some help. Spend as much time on deck in the fresh air as you can, with your eyes on the horizon. Standing up or lying down seem to help more than sitting does. Nibbling crackers to keep something in your stomach may also help, although you should avoid anything that may cause your stomach to rebel, such as spicy food. Drink lots of water to stay well hydrated.

If necessary, you can buy over-the-counter medications to ease your symptoms. Talk to your doctor and purchase the medication before you leave. You may also find that natural remedies, such as those containing ginger, or pressure patches may help.

STAYING SAFE

Any time that you bring human beings together, you unfortunately have the potential for crimes such as theft. As I mentioned earlier, being on a cruise ship is no different from being on land in this respect. The chances that you'll run into a problem are very slim, but you still need to use common sense to protect yourself and your belongings.

Many ships offer small safes in each cabin, which you should use for items that you regularly need access to, such as your passport and cash. I don't recommend taking valuable items such as jewellery with you on your cruise or any other vacation, but if you do have something particularly precious, keep it in the ship's main safe, available through the reception desk.

If you're uncomfortable about any situation on board, whether it's a potential safety hazard or another passenger's behaviour, bring it to the attention of the ship's personnel right away. They'll find the right crew member for you to speak to about the problem.

Although it's tempting to just "let go and celebrate" on a cruise (after all, you don't have to drive home!), it's best not to overindulge in alcohol-based drinks. This is partially for your own safety. There have been occasional unfortunate situations where passengers have fallen overboard, and on a large ship the fall alone can injure you or worse. You also want your legs to be steady in case of slight rolls or sways in the ship's movement. And finally, you don't want to be taken advantage of by someone, which can happen more easily if you're under the influence.

I SPENT **HOW** MUCH?

Since many of your shipboard expenditures aren't cash transactions—they're simply billed to your shipboard account—they can add up with frightening speed. Shore excursions, drinks in the lounge, photos from the ship's photographer, spa services, premium restaurants or snack bars, phone calls, checking your e-mail, shopping on board... they're all extra. Make sure you know what's included in the cruise and what's not, and keep track of what you're spending so that settling the bill at the end of the cruise isn't a big shock.

Setting up a shipboard account is a requirement, by the way. You either provide your credit card on arrival, or give a cash deposit. You'll usually receive your bill the night before you leave the ship. Check it carefully, and deal with any inaccurate charges right away. Just as with hotel and car rental bills, mistakes do happen.

Travel Best Bet!
The Bon Voyage parties typically held on the top deck the day you set sail are great fun, as most people are in the mood to celebrate the start of their vacation. Just remember that the fun, fluffy drinks with umbrellas that the waiters are handing out are not free. Many people are quite taken aback when they realize that those sweet drinks cost $15 each. They can put a really sour note on the cruise if you're not aware!

TIPPING THE BALANCE

Tipping and gratuities are common areas of concern for cruise passengers. Your cruise line will let you know what their policy is, but the usual guidelines are between US$10 and US$15 per passenger per day. Many cruise lines are replacing the expectation for tipping, however, with a flat service charge that they add to your shipboard account. In some cases, you can adjust the amount, but in others it's a fixed fee. Find out which policy your cruise line follows and you won't go wrong.

Land Ho: Disembarking

I have to admit that the process of getting thousands of people off a large cruise ship can seem rather a "hurry up and wait" situation. The cruise ship will tell you when and where to assemble before disembarking, but you should be prepared to wait for a while in that location. You rarely get to proceed immediately off the ship. Bring along a book or something else to occupy your time. If you have a tight connection, let staff know. Otherwise, this is one occasion for which I advise you to plan on arriving later rather than earlier. If your time window is 8 to 10 a.m., for example, head to the lounge at 9:45.

Travel Best Bet!
Many of our clients make the classic mistake of getting up early on the last day to have breakfast, and then leave their cabins with all their belongings. They end up waiting for two to three hours in the ship's common areas—sometimes sitting on the floor because of all the other passengers waiting there, too—before they can actually disembark. You don't want to be late, of course,

but this is one time when being early won't necessarily pay. The only reason to get to the common areas early would be to get a more comfortable seat, hopefully by a window so that you can watch what's happening on the dock or in the harbour. Otherwise, wait it out in the comfort of your cabin for as long as you possibly can.

Delays can happen, especially if you have to clear customs and immigration as you leave the ship. For this reason, it's a good idea to build in a decent window of time between your ship's expected arrival in port and your flight out of the nearest airport. If it's going to be too tight to be reasonable, opt for a hotel stay in port that night and fly out first thing the next morning.

CLAIRE'S BEST BETS FOR CRUISES

- Time spent researching your destination and the cruise ships that visit there will never be wasted. It's important to find a ship that fits your travel preferences.

- A cruise-qualified travel agent can help find the best cruise for you.

- If you don't like lots of people around you, choose a small-ship cruise.

- Book early for the best prices and best choices of ships, departures, and cabins.

- Consider upgrading your cabin to a balcony if privacy and having a view are important to you.

- Read the cruise ship's literature carefully to find out how your ship handles dining, tipping, and clothing issues.

- Pay as much—if not more—attention to health and safety on your cruise vacation as you would at home.

- Build plenty of time into your itinerary between your flight arrival and your ship's departure, and your ship's arrival and your flight home.

- Consider a hotel night's stay if the schedule's too tight on either end.

Chapter 8

On the Road: Renting a Vehicle

The Case for Rentals

For many trips, renting a vehicle is the only way to go. It gets you to places that public transportation can't reach easily, and it lets you travel at your own pace and change your itinerary on a whim. Even when you're travelling in your own backyard, it can work to your advantage to rent a vehicle. It saves wear and tear on your own vehicle, ensures that you have a nearly new vehicle that's less likely to break down, and even gives you a chance to try out a type of vehicle that you may be considering purchasing. It can also give you more room than your current vehicle, which makes all the difference if you have children, or if grandparents or friends are coming along for the ride.

Travel Best Bet!
Clients who are planning a trip to Europe often ask whether it's better to rent a vehicle or to take the train. Many of them have nostalgic ideas about backpacking through Europe, using a Eurailpass to keep travel expenses down on the rail systems. Very often, though, the passes are more expensive than renting a car. The train has an advantage if you want to sleep on board (overnighting on long trips, for example, between Paris and Rome), if you're a nervous driver, or if you love the social nature of train travel. If you don't mind driving, however—and especially if there are two of you, one to drive and one to navigate—driving can give you more

*flexibility and (even with fuel factored in) better value.
If you're unsure about driving in the cities, you can
always park the car for the day in an outlying town (or
at an airport) and take a train or bus into the city. You
may also want to consider renting a GPS system, which
many car rental agencies now offer for a small fee.*

Deals on Wheels: Making the Reservation

Don't, whatever you do, attempt to make any sense out of car rental rates. You'll
need a vacation just to recover from the effort. Instead, find out whether your
workplace or any of your associations (such as auto clubs and university alumni
organizations) or frequent flyer programs offer you discount opportunities on
car rentals. Then check the Internet to start researching rates. This gives you a
chance to determine whether it's worth using your discounts (which are usually
specific to certain companies), or whether you could get a better deal going
through a different rental company.

Of course, you can also book vehicle rentals through a travel agent who may
be able to find deals that aren't available elsewhere. The agent may also have
access to money-saving package deals that combine a flight and a rental, or
accommodation and a rental.

Like airline tickets, vehicle rental rates bow to the law of supply and demand.
If you book further ahead, when more vehicles are still available, rates tend to be
lower than if you try to book at the last minute. If you book ahead of time, your
rate will also be guaranteed, even if rates increase closer to your departure time.

When you're trying to judge rates, make sure that you're comparing apples
to apples. Vehicle rentals come with many hidden surcharges and extra fees, so
don't compare one company's all-inclusive rate with another company's bare-
bones rate. Extra charges can include airport pick-up fees, fees for dropping off
in a different location than pick-up, taxes, insurance, fuel, and additional driver
premiums.

To keep costs down, it's best to opt for the smallest vehicle that will comfortably carry you, your travelling companions, and your luggage. While this may be
smaller than you're used to, keep in mind that a smaller vehicle in places like
Europe gives you an advantage when you're parking or driving on narrow country roads. And it's not unusual to receive a free upgrade when you pick up the
car, because the sub-compact and compact categories tend to be most popular.
If the agency doesn't have any vehicles left in the category you've requested,
they'll give you a larger car at no extra charge.

When you make the reservation, note your confirmation number. If you've
opted for a pre-paid rental voucher, check all the details as soon as it arrives to

avoid any nasty surprises when you pick up the car. Ensure the dates are correct, that all insurance coverages are noted and explained, and that the pick-up location and procedures are clearly stated. Also ensure that you've given the rental car company your flight itinerary (they usually ask for your arrival flight time and airline) so that if you're delayed, they'll know to make arrangements for you to pick up the car after hours if necessary.

You should also ask where to find the rental agency's counter. Sometimes it's inside the airport, but it may be at a satellite location that's linked to the airport terminal by shuttle bus. Find out if you need to call for the shuttle, when it operates, and where it picks you up. Also ask whether the rental includes free roadside assistance. If it doesn't, check whether your local automobile association would cover you, and sign up if this would be cheaper than opting for paid roadside assistance through the rental agency.

Travel Best Bet!
Never assume that you can simply walk off the plane and hop right into a rental vehicle if you haven't pre-booked one. Rental agencies may not have a huge pool of vehicles at their disposal, especially at busy airports or during busy travel periods. In some cases, particularly in Europe, they may only retain enough cars at the airport to fulfill pre-bookings.

Fees, Fees, and More Fees

Vehicle rental agencies are notorious for finding novel ways to boost your bill. (They even give hotels a run for their money in this respect.) Here are a few that you may encounter.

AIRPORT SURCHARGES

Picking up or dropping off a vehicle at an airport generally means that you'll pay an airport surcharge. If you want to save some money, find out if it would be convenient for you to pick up the car from a downtown location or from near your hotel. If your schedule allows it, and it won't cost you much to get to the agency's location (there may be a free shuttle to your hotel), it can be cheaper to do it this way. However, if taxis or significant schedule hassles are involved, it may be cheaper—in terms of dollars and/or time—to simply pay for the airport's premium location.

THE QUESTION OF FUEL

You'll usually have a choice of at least two fuelling options when you pick up the car: fill it yourself and bring it back with a full tank, or let the rental agency fill it. The latter sounds convenient, but the agencies often charge exorbitant rates if they have to fill up the gas tank on your behalf. Consumer demand has now added a third option to many of the fuel plans: you pre-pay for a tank of gas when you pick up the car. With this option, you don't have to worry about finding a gas station just before you drop off the car, and the gas often comes at a lower price than the other two options.

Whichever option you go for, make sure that it's noted correctly on the rental contract before you leave with the car, and stick with that option. If you don't, you could be in for some hefty fees, or you could even end up paying for gas that you don't get to use.

UNLIMITED MILEAGE

Many rental agreements automatically provide unlimited mileage. Others, however, limit the distance you can drive, and will charge you a fee for any distance in excess of the limit. Always check to make sure that you have the unlimited option if you need it.

EXTRA AMENITIES

Extras such as infant and child car seats, cellphones, GPS systems, and roof racks will all add extra costs to your rental bill. If you need any of these items, be sure to reserve them when you reserve the vehicle as they may not be available if you ask for them when you arrive. If you're travelling with children, also check the rules for using car seats and booster seats in the country you're visiting to ensure that you can comply with them.

ADDITIONAL DRIVERS

The first driver on a rental vehicle is usually "included" in the price, but if you want any additional people to be authorized to drive the vehicle, there's often a fee. It's a good idea to put the extra drivers on the policy officially, even though it can cost more. If they're caught driving when they're not authorized to—for example, if they're involved in an accident—it will void your insurance coverage. This could leave you and the driver open to legal action, and to huge bills.

CAR RENTAL FOR THE YOUNG AND OLD

Because younger and older drivers are perceived to be greater accident risks than other drivers, make sure you let the rental agency know on booking if any of the drivers will be under 25 or over 65. Many simply won't rent to under-25s unless there's a special circumstance that gives them an edge: if they're military or government employees, for example, or if their company has a corporate account with the agency.

You can expect the rental agency to check the driving background of a younger or older driver, and to be more likely to refuse to rent to them if their record isn't clean. If you're an older driver, you may even want to ask your doctor for a letter confirming that you're in good health and able to drive without any restrictions.

Even when a younger driver is allowed to rent a vehicle, expect to pay extra fees and more expensive insurance. Insurance may also be more expensive for drivers over 65. If this is the case, you may want to seriously consider adding a rental vehicle clause to your personal insurance as a less expensive way to provide the coverage you need.

Vehicle Rental Insurance

Ah, the insurance question. Figuring out what, if any, of the rental agency's extra insurance coverage options you need can be a bit of a nightmare. Rental agency staff can be quite pushy when it comes to encouraging you to purchase the extra plans, which can cost as much as US$15 or US$20 a day. They'll give you all kinds of worst-case scenarios, often letting fear determine your purchase.

Your best strategy is to know which coverage you need and which coverage you don't need before you even step foot in the agency's office to pick up your vehicle. First, check your own vehicle insurance policy. If you've purchased the option for rental or "non-owned" vehicle coverage, your regular insurance will likely cover you while you're driving the rental. It's an excellent idea to call your insurance agent to find out if you have this coverage and exactly what it covers; and, if you don't have it, what it would cost to get it. It may work out to be less expensive to have your own insurance cover you for an entire year than to purchase a rental agency's coverage for a week.

Also check your credit card coverage. Many gold and platinum cards offer some kind of insurance coverage when you charge the cost of the rental to that card. It's very important to check the fine print, however, or to call the card company, because there are exclusions and limitations. You need to know what they are before you can make an informed decision.

The following are the most likely insurance plans that a rental agency will offer you.

LOSS (OR COLLISION) DAMAGE WAIVER (LDW)

This insurance means that you won't be responsible for damage to the vehicle in the event of an accident, and it may be covered through your auto insurance policy or your credit card. If you're already covered, you don't need the rental agency's plan. A "partial collision damage waiver" generally means that the rental agency's plan would cover you for any deductible that your other insurance wouldn't.

In Europe, many vehicle rental packages come with LDW. It's part of the package price, whether you need it or not.

SUPPLEMENTAL LIABILITY INSURANCE

This type of insurance covers the driver if they're at fault in an accident in which someone is injured. Your auto insurance policy also often covers this, but do check the maximum limit. Some areas have different minimum coverages that you need to carry, so if your personal policy has a lower limit than the area in which you're driving, you may need the rental agency's coverage to top you up.

TRIP CANCELLATION AND MEDICAL INSURANCE

Coverages offered at car rental agencies for trip cancellation or personal medical insurance tend to be much more expensive than those offered elsewhere. If you need these policies, research your options and take them out before you leave on your trip. They're widely available from many outlets, including, of course, your travel agency.

PERSONAL PROPERTY INSURANCE

This covers your personal property while it's in the rental vehicle. Your home insurance will often cover property that's off-site, so it's always worth checking your policy before you purchase additional coverage.

Picking Up the Vehicle

Make sure you have your driver's licence and credit card with you when you pick up the car. If you're picking up an international rental, also have your international driver's licence. (See "On the Road, with International Driving Permits" in Chapter 1, Planning for Paradise.)

Your credit card is essential because most rental agencies will charge a deposit to the card, or at least take an imprint of it, to protect themselves in case you damage the vehicle or don't return it on time. Expect the deposit to be at least the rental cost, and usually slightly more. Of course, if you've pre-paid the rental cost the deposit shouldn't be quite as much, but many agencies will still charge you one.

Some rental agencies maintain check-in counters at the airport while others send a shuttle bus to the terminals regularly to pick up their customers. Just watch for the signs. If the airport is small, or you've arrived at off-peak hours, you may need to call the agency to request the bus.

If you realize you're going to arrive late, do whatever you can to notify the rental agency that you're still en route, and that you still need the vehicle. Ask what you should do if you arrive later than the regular opening hours of the rental agency. (Some agencies will leave a staff member on duty if they know that you're coming after hours.) Your worst-case scenario is not being able to pick up the car until the agency office opens again the next morning. In this case—if you haven't pre-paid your rental and there's no cancellation fee for your reservation—see if there's a rental agency in the airport that's open and has cars available. It may be more expensive than your original reservation, but it will get you on the road as planned.

Once you're at the check-in counter, read the rental agreement very, very carefully before you sign or initial anywhere on the paper. Once you've signed it, it becomes an official contract.

Pay attention to any rules about where you can take the vehicle. Some can't be driven across state or international lines; others aren't allowed on dirt or gravel roads. Always be sure you understand where you can drive the car because if you stray outside those boundaries you'll likely void your insurance coverages and possibly be hit with hefty fines. Also be aware that many vehicles are now non-smoking. Lighting up will net you a nasty cleaning bill when you return the vehicle.

Make sure you know the rental agency's 24-hour emergency phone number, and reconfirm whether the rental includes roadside assistance.

After you've signed the contract, you'll head out to pick up your vehicle. Don't drive away just yet, however. Most rental agencies will give you a separate sheet that lists any existing damage to the car, and gives you spaces to list any damage that's not noted on the sheet. Go over the interior and exterior of the vehicle with the rental agent present, looking for any kind of damage, including stains on the upholstery. The rental agency will do the same thing when you return the vehicle, and unless you've noted the damage before you leave, you could be charged for it even if you didn't cause it. Ouch! Common damages to look for include scratches around keyholes, scrapes on tires and hubcaps, and rock chips in windshields.

Once you're in the vehicle and ready to go, spend some time adjusting the mirrors and the seats, and familiarizing yourself with all the controls, including headlights and windshield wipers. This is especially important if you've rented a vehicle with a standard transmission and you're more accustomed to driving an automatic.

Travel Best Bet!
A friend of mine picked up a standard-transmission rental car at Heathrow Airport, in England. Because England is "left-hand" drive (that is, on the opposite side of the road from North America), she wisely spent some time driving around the rental agency's parking lot to get used to having the gearshift on the opposite side. She also tried to find reverse gear while still in the parking lot—but no matter what she did, she just couldn't get the car into gear. Finally, she gave up and asked for help. It turned out that there was a small handle below the gearshift knob that she needed to pull up on at the same time as shifting the gear lever. Good thing she checked!

Staying Safe on the Road

The same safety rules apply when driving rental vehicles as apply at home: wear your seatbelt, drive defensively, use caution, obey the rules of the road, lock your doors as soon as you get in, never leave the keys in the car, and don't leave any valuables in view. There are, however, some additional factors to consider when you're in an unfamiliar place driving an unfamiliar car.

First, ask if the vehicle has airbags, especially if you have children in the car. Children under 12 should ride in the back seat anyway, but this becomes essential if the vehicle has airbags. If they're deployed, they can seriously injure or even kill small children in the front passenger seat. Never, ever put babies in the front seat.

Also, ask about anti-lock brakes. These create a "pumping" action that will reduce the likelihood that the brakes will lock up and cause a skid. You should never pump the brake pedal yourself if the vehicle has anti-lock brakes.

In many areas, you also want to avoid identifying the vehicle as a rental (this makes it a more likely target for theft or carjacking), so it shouldn't display any stickers from the agency. Researching your destination ahead of time will let you know if this is an issue.

Ensure that you know where you're going when you leave the rental agency's lot. Although staff are usually happy to give you directions and some basic maps, it helps if you've obtained detailed maps ahead of time. Websites such as Map-Quest (www.mapquest.com) can also provide excellent driving instructions between destinations. It's really worthwhile to spend some time at your computer before you leave, printing out maps and directions. If the vehicle comes with a GPS system, program the coordinates of your destination before you leave the parking lot.

Use your common sense about where you park or stop to fill up with gas. Make sure you choose well-lit, busy areas.

If another car or someone on the road indicates for you to pull over (bumping your car from behind, for example)—don't. Stay calm, keep driving, and head to the nearest well-lit, busy location. This also applies if you're having trouble with the vehicle. As long as the vehicle is still driveable, don't stop on the road or on the shoulder. Also, although most of us will automatically want to stop and help someone on the road who needs assistance, this could be a ploy. Again, keep driving to a well-lit place. If you have a cellphone with you, call 9-1-1 (or the local equivalent: something else you should research before leaving) and explain the situation, and ask for help. If you pass a police vehicle along the way, try to get their attention.

If you're ever physically threatened, however, simply give up the car. It's not worth the risk to you and your family's safety. And don't forget that everything I've mentioned here really is just the same kind of common-sense precaution that you'd take at home, too.

How to Handle Breakdowns and Damage

In the case of an accident, you obviously need to focus on any injuries before worrying about the vehicle. As soon as possible, however, notify the rental agency of the situation.

If the vehicle breaks down or there's a non-injury accident, you need to notify the rental agency immediately. Most major agencies have roadside assistance that they can send out, even if it's only a tow truck. If the breakdown isn't your fault, they should provide you with a replacement vehicle as soon as possible, at no cost to you. If you've caused the breakdown (for example, putting diesel gas into an unleaded engine, which is difficult but not impossible to do in some cars, especially if you're in vacation mode), expect that you'll be hit with fees for a replacement vehicle, possibly at the rental agency's highest rate.

With smaller rental agencies, you may have to arrange for the vehicle to be repaired locally, but they'll let you know what your options are when you call. If the breakdown wasn't your fault, the agency will need to reimburse you when you return the car. Otherwise, you'll need to start the process of claiming through your insurance coverage(s).

Whatever the situation, be sure to document everything that happened and take photographs if possible. In an accident, that means obtaining all the insurance, registration, and licence details of the other drivers, and the exact details of what happened, as well as when, where, and how. If the police come to the scene, ensure that you receive a copy of the police report if possible, or at least obtain the contact information of the police officers so that you can obtain a report later.

Be aware that rental agencies often consider certain actions to be violations of your contract. These include driving under the influence; allowing an unauthorized driver to drive; leaving the windows, doors, or trunk unlocked; and leaving the keys in the ignition when you're parked. These will void your insurance coverages at the very least, and may expose you to fees or fines as well.

Returning the Vehicle

Unless you want to be charged for an extra day's rental, make sure that you return the vehicle by the same time of day that you picked it up. For example, if you picked up your car at 9 a.m., return it before 9 a.m. on the day you're dropping it off. Rental agencies give very little grace on this. If you return it beyond that last 24-hour period you'll most likely be charged for the extra time. If you've chosen the self-fill fuel option, make your last stop before drop-off at the nearest gas station. Forgetting to fill up, or not leaving enough time to stop to fill up, means that you'll be charged for any gas the rental agency has to put into the vehicle's tank to fill it up.

Also keep in mind that if you've received any parking or traffic tickets, they'll follow you home. The rental agency will simply forward them on to you for payment, or will bill your credit card for them, so don't take any chances. In some cases, tickets received elsewhere can affect your insurance or driving record at home, too. (Certain US states and Canadian provinces have an "exchange" agreement, for example.)

RETURNING A DAMAGED VEHICLE

If the rental vehicle has been damaged in any way, you should already have notified the rental agency, but be sure to draw attention to the damage on its return. You don't want to be accused of failing to inform them. Bring all the appropriate documentation or paperwork regarding the damage, but don't just hand it over. Take copies of it so that you have a record, too. It's also a good idea to take photographs of the damage, in case you need to refer to them later.

Take down the name and contact information of the rental agency personnel with whom you're dealing. If you haven't already done so, contact the primary insurance agency (your personal policy's provider, your credit card company, or the rental agency's insurance provider). Make sure that you fill in all the paperwork that's required, and file your claims within any time limit that your policies may specify.

Roadworthy Notes

Always check the local driving customs and regulations of the countries you'll be visiting. The most obvious difference will be those that drive on the left, instead of on the right (as we do in North America). Examples of left-hand-drive countries include Australia, the Bahamas, Bermuda, British Virgin Islands, Cyprus, Hong Kong, India, Ireland, Japan, New Zealand, Singapore, South Africa, St. Lucia, and, of course, the United Kingdom.

Other issues to check include parking (in Britain, for example, you don't need to park in the direction of travel), passing (again, in Britain, you're not allowed to pass a vehicle by driving in the slow lane—you need to use the fast lane for overtaking slower vehicles), and even idling (rules in Germany, for example, are quite strict about the length of time you can let the vehicle idle).

Also find out when gas stations are usually open, and whether the country has 24-hour gas stations (which are often automated, which means that you'll insert your credit card right at the pump in order to start the refuelling process and pay for the fuel).

CLAIRE'S BEST BETS FOR RENTING A VEHICLE

- Book early for the best rates, and watch for extra charges such as airport and additional driver premiums.

- Take note of your fuel option and stick to it.

- Check your own insurance and credit card coverages so that you'll know what, if any, additional insurance you need.

- Always look over the vehicle for damage before you drive it off the lot.

- Drive with due care and attention. Stay safe.

- Don't stop on the road unless you absolutely have to, and call the police if you need help.

- Notify the rental agency immediately in the event of breakdown, accident, or damage.

- Return the vehicle before the time of day when you picked it up to avoid extra charges.

Chapter 9
Lodgings: Where to Lay Your Head

What's Your Style?

Choosing the right lodgings has make-or-break potential for your trip. It's really difficult to keep putting on a happy, positive face if your room is uncomfortable, noisy, dirty, or otherwise not up to par. Part of getting the accommodation equation right is knowing what type of accommodation suits you best. Here's a quick rundown of your major options to give you an idea of where you might be happiest.

HOSTELS

Hostels used to be the last refuge of the money-strapped backpacking crowd, and the facilities reflected that—fairly spartan, and definitely shared with your fellow travellers. Well, hostels aren't what they used to be. They're still fairly communal and inexpensive, but many are also very comfortable, offering family accommodation and a range of local activities that you can join in.

MOTELS

These arrived on the scene thanks to our love affair with the automobile. All you have to do is drive up and walk in through your own front door. Often one- or two-storey buildings, they're generally clean, if perhaps a little basic in their furnishings and amenities at the lower end of the cost spectrum. Add a little more money, however, and you can often get a pool, decent furnishings, and on-site dining. They may not be luxurious, but they can be great value.

HOTELS

Hotels come in all kinds, from budget chains to five-star luxury. You generally get what you pay for, especially when it comes to service. The higher-end hotels really know how to keep their customers happy. Depending on the hotel, it may come with a pool, spa, fitness centre, business centre, conference and meeting areas, and shops. One sector that's relatively new on the market is the "boutique" hotel. These set themselves apart with unique interior design that often includes original art. See below for more on hotels.

BED & BREAKFAST INNS (B&Bs)

The B&Bs that are ubiquitous in Europe have now cracked the North American scene as well. They are typically in someone's home, where the owners have turned between one and three rooms into guest accommodation. While it was once standard to have shared bathrooms that were down the hallway, most B&Bs—even in Europe—have now realized that people really, really want their own "loo." The price is usually quite reasonable, especially in areas where hotels are expensive, and, as you'd expect from the name, it includes breakfast. By their nature, they're not as private as hotels, but they're great if you're a sociable creature and love meeting fellow guests and your hosts (who can be wonderful sources of that most precious commodity when you're travelling, local information).

COUNTRY INNS

These tend to be more upscale than B&Bs, but often have a similar social feel to them, especially if they're owner-operated. They can range from small and quaint to large and richly decorated, but will likely have a strong focus on local or on-property activities (such as hiking and antiquing). They're often historic or older buildings, a characteristic that adds charm and personality.

ALL-INCLUSIVE RESORTS

Ah, the all-inclusive. The very word conjures up images of sand, sea, and fruity drinks with umbrellas (but remember to skip the ice cubes!). All-inclusive resorts are a relatively new phenomenon, but they've been growing in popularity over the last 15 years. Although they can be found in many countries around the world (e.g., the Club Med chain), the majority are still found in Mexico and the Caribbean. If you're looking to get away from it all these can be an excellent option, and very good value. You can literally eat, sleep, and play there very happily without ever stepping foot outside the property. Those who value getting out and exploring the local area, however, may find them a little artificial. The key to happiness at an all-inclusive is knowing exactly what's included, where the resort is (how close to the beach/ski hill, for example), how big it is, and to whom it caters (couples, singles, families, partiers, etc.).

VILLA/HOUSE/CONDO RENTALS

The complete opposite of staying at an all-inclusive resort is renting a private villa, house, or condo. You can rent anything from a small studio apartment to a grand villa, generally by the week, and in return, you have a base among the local people and culture, and a chance to cook your own meals rather than paying to eat out all the time. This option tends to be more private because you have the place to yourself and there's probably maid service only once a week (unless you've requested something more frequent). For the independent sort that love living like the local people do, this is ideal. It's not as good if your itinerary is far-ranging, but it's well suited to those who want to explore one area in depth.

UNIQUE STAYS

Have you ever dreamed about a lighthouse, a dude ranch, a castle, or even caves and tree houses? If you can dream about it, you can probably stay in it, somewhere in the world. You may pay a little more for the privilege, but it will definitely be a watercooler-worthy story when you get back to work!

To find the unique stay that fits your dreams, start by checking with heritage associations: in many countries, they offer quirky vacation rental properties. You can also try searching on the Internet for certain keywords (such as "Canada lighthouse vacation rental"). Talk to your travel agent, too, as they often hear about fun alternatives.

Swap Meet! Exchanging Your Home

The home exchange option merits a section all its own, partly because of its growing popularity, and partly because it goes so far beyond simply renting a room. It means that you actually switch houses with someone, often someone you don't even know. Scary? Maybe a little, because there are numerous un-known factors. But many people who've opted to trade houses rave about the experience. At its best, it can be like coming home, but in a brand new, exciting place. Plus, it seriously reduces your accommodation costs and can be a source of home decor ideas if you're looking to make your own place a little more exotic! At its worst, you could come home to a house that's dirty or damaged, or find that you've been robbed. Very few instances of the worst-case scenario happen, but you do need to protect yourself by doing your research and working through reputable agencies.

There are a number of directories and agencies that list homeowners willing to exchange their homes with other people. It's best to work with an agency that has a good track record and history in the industry, and that offers support such as written agreements for the home exchangers. These agreements should cover issues such as exactly what's being exchanged (for example, some home exchanges also cover vehicles), maintenance responsibilities (if it's a month-long exchange, someone's going to have to mow the lawn), whether the home allows smoking or not, any additional insurance that may be required, and what happens if one party has to cancel. You may wish to seek the advice of your lawyer about this contract to make sure that it's enforceable and legal.

Generally, you'll exchange e-mails or calls with prospective exchangers to find an exchanger and a home that's a good fit for you. Keep in mind that the exchanges are usually done at the same time, so that you're literally swapping homes, but some exchangers prefer to host each other. This second option can be a little tricky. If you end up not liking the other party, you're stuck with them for one or more weeks. But if it's a good match, you've just made some brand new friends.

Before you leave your own home it's a good idea to put away items that have high monetary or sentimental value: for example, in safety deposit boxes, in a storage area, or at a friend's house. It's unlikely that a home exchange will result in theft, but think how badly both families would feel if something valuable was broken or damaged. You also need to verify that your home insurance covers you for someone else staying in your home, in terms of liability and property/contents loss, and that your vehicle insurance will cover another driver.

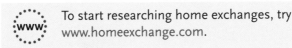

To start researching home exchanges, try www.homeexchange.com.

Hot Tips for Hotels

Once you've had a taste of the hotel life, it can be difficult to go home again. After all, it's a lovely luxury to know that someone else is taking care of all the household chores, from cleaning to cooking. All you have to do is enjoy! Here are a few tips to help you get the most from your stay.

CHOICES, CHOICES: MAKING THE BEST ONE

It can be difficult to pick a hotel from a brochure or an Internet site. As anyone who has ever bought or sold a home will tell you, photos can be taken from angles that give misleading views. Descriptions may also be inflated or outdated, again giving you misleading information. Here are a few tips to help you choose a hotel that will make you happy.

- Don't rely on brochures or Internet pictures and descriptions. Verify the hotel's details, and watch for phrases such as "near the beach," "within walking distance of shops," and "family friendly." Ask for specifics, and better yet, figure them out for yourself (an Internet search, particularly if you use something like MapQuest, might show you the exact location of the hotel in relation to what's around it).

- Check travel guidebooks (more than one, if possible) to see if the hotel is listed, and type the hotel's name into an Internet search engine. If it comes up on a site such as www.tripadvisor.com, www.hotelshark.com, or www.igougo.com you can see what other visitors have to say about it. These three sites do their best to avoid fake reviews, so they're relatively reliable. Your search may also reveal travel articles about the property from newspapers and magazines.

- You can also ask friends, family, and colleagues for recommendations, but make sure that your vacation goals are similar. If you're looking for quiet, a party-hearty traveller may not give you a recommendation that's a good fit.

- Read all the fine print. Look for hidden surcharges such as daily activity fees, and if it's billed as all-inclusive, find out exactly what's included and what's not.

- Don't trust "star" rating systems unless they come from a recognizable and trustworthy international organization: "three-star" in one country can be what you'd consider "two-star" at home. The American Automobile Association's "diamond" ratings can generally be relied upon.

- Make sure you understand all the room costs, including surcharges and all taxes.

LET'S MAKE A DEAL! GETTING THE BEST PRICE $

If you're looking to save money, opt for weekend stays in big cities. Many of the larger hotels cater to business clients during the week but have problems filling rooms on Friday and Saturday nights. Try to travel during shoulder seasons to avoid peak season prices, and consider hotels that are a little farther away from tourist attractions or the city centre. Also look for hotels that offer free services, such as breakfasts or shuttle transportation to the ski hill.

The Internet is a great place to shop around and compare prices, but don't rely on the sites that offer access to many hotels. You can often find better deals by checking the hotel's own website (look for anything that says "packages" or "specials") or by calling the hotel direct—not on its toll-free reservation line, but on its direct number—and simply asking if they're offering any deals. Remember, if you don't ask you don't get, and the worst they can say is "no."

Keep an eye on your credit card statements, too, for special discount offers. Automobile and alumni associations may be worth checking as they negotiate member discounts with a number of outlets, including hotels. You can also look for coupons and special offers on the Internet, either with a general search or by going directly to the local tourist association or visitor's bureau website. Remember, too, that travel agents receive special incentives and packages all the time, and may be able to obtain a great deal, an upgrade, or a special bonus for you.

Do book early. Last-minute discounts, especially for popular destinations, are becoming harder to find. Don't forget to ask for a special discount or package deal. You'll be amazed at what's available if you just ask. And ALWAYS get a confirmation number for everything that you do, whether it's making a reservation or cancelling one. Print off any e-mail confirmation and take it with you.

GETTING A ROOM WITH A VIEW

If you're looking for a romantic getaway or a stress-reducing vacation, the last thing you want is a cramped room in a noisy area of the hotel. Your best strategy for getting a room that's right for you is to decide in advance exactly what you want and then compare it to what the hotel offers. For example, if a king-size bed and non-smoking room are absolute musts, put them at the top of your list. If you desperately want a room with a view, write that down, too. Once you have your list, check to see what the hotel offers. Then call the hotel directly to book as far in advance of your travel as possible.

Don't use the toll-free reservation number for chain hotels, by the way. That's likely to be a call centre, and may be far, far away from the hotel itself. You need to speak to a member of the hotel staff who's actually familiar with the property. Also, avoid calling when they're likely busy checking guests in or out (early mornings and mid- to late afternoons).

Once you have them on the phone, be specific about your requests. Let them know that you need a whirlpool bathtub or a room that's nowhere near the property's casino. Also, if this is a special occasion, be sure to let the reservations agent know. You may not always get everything you want, but you'll stand a better chance by asking in advance than by waiting until you arrive at the front desk. If you've requested something, have been assured that it's available, and then find it's not delivered, the hotel should be prepared to switch your room or offer a partial refund or other bonus to make up for your disappointment. It helps to note the person's name to whom you're speaking, and to ask for written (perhaps e-mailed) confirmation of the details that you've requested.

Travel Best Bet!
A common mistake that I've seen over the years is clients flying overnight and thinking that they can have their hotel room right away. Remember that the check-in time for most hotels worldwide is 3 or 4 p.m., although it does vary between hotels, as do check-out times. You can often leave your luggage with reception staff before checking in or after checking out, however. Just ask.

NIGHT NIGHT, SLEEP TIGHT: GETTING A DECENT SLEEP IN A HOTEL

I love my sleep immensely, so over the years I've gathered a few tips and tricks that will help you get a decent sleep when you're on the road, whether you're taking an afternoon nap or disappearing into dreamland overnight.

First, your chances of getting a decent sleep increase exponentially with the quality of the hotel. Construction is usually better in higher-quality hotels, meaning there'll be less noise transmission between rooms, and—hopefully—guests will be less likely to disturb others and staff will be more responsive in case they do. This isn't a clear guarantee, though. Just recently, a group of university students caused a huge number of problems for a very high-quality hotel in a mountain resort area. The students have since apologized, but that doesn't help the guests they disturbed with their antics. In this case, though, the hotel's staff took the whole issue very seriously, and tried actively to deal with the problem for their other guests.

When you're booking your room, ask specifically where it is. If you want peace and quiet, be sure to ask for it. Avoid rooms near noisy areas such as swimming pools, casinos, restaurants, and nightclubs, and avoid elevators, ice machines, and delivery access points.

Travel Best Bet!
I really love my own pillow. If I'm staying somewhere for more than a week, I take it with me as carry-on—it even makes the flight more comfortable. Sweet dreams!

To get ready for sleep, close your curtains, put out the "do not disturb" sign, and set the interior door lock (the one that you use when you're in the room). If the plumbing's noisy, close the bathroom door (place a towel at the bottom of the door if there's a big gap there). Make the room as much like home as possible. Put a glass of water on the night table, set the radio or TV to "sleep" mode, add extra pillows or blankets—whatever will make you most comfortable.

A sleep mask and earplugs can be very handy, but try them out at home before the trip so that you get used to them.

If, despite your best efforts, a party down the hall is making it impossible to sleep, start by calling the front desk and letting them know there's a problem. Ask for security to deal with the situation immediately. If there's no improvement within 30 minutes, go down to the front desk in person and ask to be switched to a quieter room immediately. It's going to be a real hassle to pack up and move, but if it means getting half a night's sleep instead of none, it may be worth it. Your other option is to ask for a different room just for that night, in which case you can leave most of your luggage in your own room and sleep in the other room. I definitely don't recommend approaching the people who are being noisy, because they're likely to be drunk and unreasonable. Don't put yourself in an unsafe situation.

If you're kept up half the night by a noisy situation that the hotel can't get under control effectively, and you've called and spoken to the front desk about it, ask to speak to the hotel's general manager the next morning. They should bend over backwards to ensure that it doesn't happen again, and they should provide at least a partial refund or some other "sweetener" to make up for your disturbed peace.

DON'T LET THE BEDBUGS BITE

Unfortunately, even the best of hotels can sometimes fall victim to what their guests bring with them—such as nasty hangers-on like bedbugs and lice— as recent newscasts have reported. Always check your hotel room when you arrive to make sure that there are no signs of bugs, including spider webs, black specks on sheets, and bug droppings in corners. If the issue is that the room hasn't been well cleaned, ask for it to be cleaned again. But if the issue is larger than that, and you suspect an insect infestation, immediately ask for another room—or find another hotel.

It can be expensive to pay twice for accommodation when you're on vacation, and, depending on the circumstances, you may not get a refund on the original hotel—but think about how much it's going to cost you in emotional wear-and-tear to stay in a place that's dirty or insect-infested, and how much it's going to cost if any of those nasty bugs hitch a ride home with you.

To avoid bringing bugs home in your luggage, use a luggage rack or put your suitcase on a table or chest of drawers where it's less likely to pick up bugs crawling along the floor. When you're not digging into your luggage, zip it up tight. If you're carrying snacks, take them out of your luggage and put them into sealed plastic containers somewhere else in the room.

If you're really concerned, when you get home leave the suitcase outside and call a local pest removal expert. They may recommend spraying the luggage and its contents, leaving it outside in below-freezing temperatures, or sealing it in a plastic bag for a couple of weeks. Wash your clothing in hot water, if possible.

If the worst happens and you wake up covered in a rash or bites, report your situation to the hotel management immediately and seek medical advice. If lice are a problem, you'll likely need to treat your hair with a de-licing shampoo. Again, it's important to talk to medical specialists and to make sure that you know exactly what you're dealing with.

 Travel Best Bet!
A friend who was travelling in a very undeveloped area was glad to find a hotel at the end of the day—but less happy when she discovered a veritable army of ants marching down the wall and across the floor. She quickly moved her backpack off the floor and gave it a good spray with the insect repellent that she'd purchased when she arrived in the country. It worked!

KEEPING COSTS DOWN

A massive bill padded with extra charges at the end of your stay is a surefire way to end your vacation on a sour note. The best way to avoid this is to be aware of all possible fees before you arrive, or at least find out about them on arrival. Don't be afraid to ask about the extras that the hotel charges. The following categories are notorious for inflated pricing.

Minibar Madness

This is the land of the US$6 soda pop and the US$4 bag of potato chips. A quick snack, and suddenly your hotel bill is nearly US$15 more expensive (remember, there's tax on those snacks!). If you don't want to use the minibar, request that it be sealed, don't accept the key for it when you arrive, or ask for it to be cleared of its contents. If you want to use the fridge for your own snacks, you could just remove the contents. In some hotels there's an electronic sensor that automatically bills your room when the minibar's contents are removed, so find out first from the front desk whether this is the case and, if so, make sure you let them know that the contents are still in the room.

Either bring snacks from home or buy them locally after you arrive to avoid falling victim to the goodies at the minibar. If you have a small fridge (even the teensy minibar fridge will work), you can keep milk and juice in it overnight for breakfast the next morning. Think of it as do-it-yourself room service! This also works well if you're travelling with children (who often can't wait to eat too long after waking) or with someone who has diabetes.

>
> *Travel Best Bet!*
> A friend recently travelled to Houston, Texas, on a
> birdwatching trip. When she checked out the continental
> breakfast that the hotel offered, it was a stunning US$15
> for coffee, a piece of fruit, and a Danish. Ouch! She
> opted instead for a friendly deli nearby that sold great
> coffee, yoghurt, fruit, and pastries—and enjoyed a
> delicious breakfast for US$5.

Room Service Splurges

You know, there's nothing like breakfast served on fine china while you're still in your fluffy hotel robe, or a piping-hot dinner wheeled in for you and your sweetie to enjoy in complete privacy. Splurging on room service can be a wonderful thing, but just be aware of how much it will cost before you indulge to avoid unpleasant surprises on checkout.

The bill will probably include the price of the food, plus a room service surcharge, plus a tip or a gratuity for the person who delivers the food. When the bill arrives, check to make sure that you've been charged for the correct items.

Extra, Extra

In-room movies, fitness-centre access, daily newspaper delivery—in many hotels these are complimentary, but sometimes they're not. Find out if there's a charge to use the outdoor BBQ that some vacation resorts make available for their guests, for example. Other services, such as yoga classes, spas, and guided activities will most likely have a fee. Know before you go!

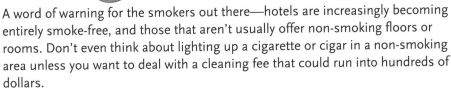

Lighting Up

A word of warning for the smokers out there—hotels are increasingly becoming entirely smoke-free, and those that aren't usually offer non-smoking floors or rooms. Don't even think about lighting up a cigarette or cigar in a non-smoking area unless you want to deal with a cleaning fee that could run into hundreds of dollars.

OOPS! HOTEL BILL MISTAKES

It's absolutely essential to read your hotel bill carefully when you check out. Many hotels now prepare the bill online or on paper and deliver it to you the night before you're due to check out. This gives you a great opportunity to go through it line by line, to make sure that all is as it should be. Think mistakes don't happen very often? You'd be wrong. One recent survey showed that almost 12 percent of bills from major hotels contained errors.

Travel Best Bet!
Find out from the hotel what information is kept on those electronic key cards that unlock your room. You may discover that there's everything from your name, address, and phone number to your credit card details. Ask front desk staff to "wipe" the card clean in front of you when you check out, or take the card with you and shred it. This personal information can be used fraudulently if it falls into the wrong hands.

First, check that the room rate is correct. Then count the number of nights that have been charged to the room to make sure that you haven't been charged for any extra nights. Also, check the extras. Make sure that there's nothing on the bill that shouldn't be there, and that any extras have been charged to you correctly.

Be sure to raise billing issues with hotel staff as soon as you find them. In particular, don't leave the front desk on checkout without resolving the issue. If the front desk staff can't solve the problem, ask to see the on-duty manager. Note the names of the people with whom you're dealing. If it's not resolved to your satisfaction, see "When It All Goes Wrong" below.

WHEN IT ALL GOES WRONG

You show up at your hotel and it's overbooked and you don't have a room. Or it's not at all what was advertised. Or it's undergoing renovations that have turned it into a construction zone. What can you do?

Overwhelmed and Overbooked

First, to avoid being "walked" to another hotel in an overbooking situation, be sure to guarantee your reservation with a credit card. Non-guaranteed reservations are generally cancelled if you don't arrive by 6 p.m., but on busy days, that can start happening as early as 4 p.m. Arrive mid-afternoon if you can. Your room may not be ready yet, but at least you stand a better chance of getting a room than if you show up in the early evening. If you'll be arriving late, call the hotel directly, let them know that you have a guaranteed reservation, and tell them what time you'll be arriving. They'll be less likely to give your room away if they're sure you're coming. If you're a member of the hotel's reward program, you're also less likely to get "bumped."

Just Not Good Enough

If there's a major problem with your hotel, with your room, or with the service that you receive, always try to resolve it on the spot. Ask to be transferred to another room or another hotel. If the hotel says that you'll be charged for your full stay whether or not you stay there, you then have to make a decision about whether the issue is serious enough to warrant the extra expense. In some cases it will be.

Whatever the situation is, make sure that you document it as clearly as possible. Take photos of the room or the hotel, note the names of the people you spoke with in trying to resolve the problem, and don't stop at the front desk staff—go right to the manager. For every problem, try to have a solution available. For example, if the room you booked isn't available, you might ask for a rate reduction and to be moved to a better room as soon as one becomes vacant. If you booked through a travel agent or tour operator, call them to see if they can assist you.

Sometimes there's nothing that you can do to resolve the situation on the spot. In this case, make sure that you write a letter of complaint as soon as you get home, and send it to the highest possible person in the hotel's hierarchy: the general manager of the hotel or of the chain that operates the hotel. Talk to your travel agent, if you have one. If you and your travel agent are having difficulty resolving the issue, there are other people you may be able to lodge a complaint with, such as the local visitor's bureau, the local government's consumer protection or tourism ministry, or even the Better Business Bureau (or equivalent).

 Travel Best Bet!
It's a good idea to check for local complaint procedures, too. In Spain, for example, hotels have a special complaints form, called a libro de reclamaciones, *which you use to formally file a complaint with the* Dirección General de Turismo, *the general tourism board.*

Of course, if you paid with a credit card, you should also notify the credit card company that you want the charge reversed. Be aware, however, that when they investigate the matter, it's going to be your word against the hotel's. Always be clear about what you were promised, and what you actually received. Attaching documentation that proves it is absolutely key.

CLAIRE'S BEST BETS FOR LODGINGS

- Know your lodging style to find the best fit.
- Research the hotel yourself. Don't rely on their brochure or Internet descriptions.
- Always call the hotel directly to get the best rates and the best rooms.
- Read the fine print, and always check for extra charges.
- Get a good night's sleep by making your room feel like home.
- Hotel bill mistakes happen. Check yours before you leave the hotel.
- If something's not right (with the hotel, with a noisy party, with your room), always complain to the front desk immediately, and then to the management.
- Document everything if there's a problem, and lodge a complaint in writing.

Chapter 10
Logistical Logic: On the Trip

Put On a Happy Face

The one thing that you can guarantee about any kind of travel is that you'll encounter some bumps along the way. Some may be tiny speed bumps that you can get over quickly, but others may be small mountains that need some work to climb over.

I mentioned earlier that the traveller's motto should be Flexible, Organized, and Prepared. That will certainly go a long way towards making your trip one that's memorable for all the right reasons, but you have to remember that it doesn't matter how organized and prepared you are, hiccups do still happen. When they do, your best approach is to keep your attitude as positive as possible under the circumstances. The person you're dealing with will often not be the person who's caused the problem, but they may just be the person who can help you solve it.

> **TBB** *Travel Best Bet!*
> *A colleague travelling on a European airline recently was asked by a flight attendant to look after a young child who was travelling alone, and who happened to be sitting near her. This was an entirely inappropriate request for the flight attendant to make, but to object to it in front of the child would have been equally inappropriate. My colleague asked the flight attendant to step to the rear of the aircraft and, once there, explained that she would not be taking responsibility for a child she didn't know. She suggested that her seat be switched, thus allowing the flight attendant to sit in the child's row whenever necessary.*

I believe that you should be a firm advocate for yourself, but in a pleasant, or at least calm, manner. I can guarantee that it will improve the situation much faster than if you lose your temper.

If you do end up facing a difficult situation on your vacation, do your best to mitigate it as quickly as possible. And don't hold a grudge. I realize that for some people (like me!) this is easier said than done. But getting angry or frustrated will just make you miserable. Do whatever you need to do (e.g., chocolate, wine, exercise) to get over the situation as quickly and painlessly as possible, and then focus on the bigger picture. Don't let one bad moment ruin the entire trip!

Also keep in mind that there's nothing worse than travelling with someone who's in a bad mood. If you can get over your frustration fairly quickly your travelling companions will thank you for it, and you'll have a better time, too.

The following sections should help you navigate many of the logistical problems or areas of concern that may come up on a trip—no matter how or where you are travelling.

The Art of Tipping

The most common questions I hear are about currency, but questions about tipping have to come in a close second. I've noticed more and more that travellers obsess over the issue of tipping, turning it into a bigger problem than it ought to be. Some clients told me not long ago that while they were on a trip to Bangkok, they found themselves with only large Thai baht bills and nothing small enough to give to a cab driver. Plus, they didn't really know how much to tip anyway, which made matters worse, so they got a car service instead. Even though the car service cost two to three times as much as a taxi, they chose it because they didn't want to worry about having to tip.

This is why I recommend that you research your destination on the Internet or e-mail your hotel and ask about the local customs before you leave, or you could even ask the hotel concierge once you arrive. Arming yourself with the right information takes a lot of the stress out of the issue. There are, however, some general rules that will keep you—and your service provider—happy both in North America and in many other parts of the world.

- If in doubt, add 10 percent. It will at least keep you out of the bad books of most wait staff and taxi drivers. But keep in mind that 15 to 20 percent for good service in restaurants (unless the menu states that service is included) and in taxis is usually reasonable.

- $1 to $2 for parking valets and "a buck a bag" for porters are also safe bets.

- $1 to $2 for door personnel who help you do things like load your luggage or hail a taxi.

- $5 to $25 for concierges who provide service beyond answering simple questions. If they can get you tickets to a local theatre or sporting event, for example, tip on the high side.

- $1 to $2 every day on the pillow or nightstand for hotel maids (place this in an envelope labelled "maid service" so that it's clear to the staff that the money is for them).

- Whenever possible, tip in the local currency.

- Keep small bills or dollar coins handy (but not too accessible to pick-pockets), so you'll have easy access to them when needed—for example, when you arrive at or leave your hotel.

Note that these are just guidelines. It's always better to find out the local customs because in some countries a service charge or gratuity is automatically added to your restaurant or hotel bill, and in other areas tipping is not only "not customary," it's considered quite rude. There are also places where leaving your tip on the table at a restaurant isn't "done"—you actually need to hand it to the server. So, a little research ahead of time can go a long way.

Remember, a tip is a way of saying, "Thanks for the service," whether it's a speedy cab or a welcoming waiter. Don't feel obligated to tip if the service was bad, and don't be shy about tipping extra if it was particularly good!

WHEN IN ROME...TIP AS THE ROMANS DO

As soon as you step out of North America, the tipping landscape changes. Sometimes, it can appear very similar to what we expect to do at home, but there are hidden traps. For example, in many areas of Europe a service charge is included in restaurant bills, which means that you wouldn't usually be expected to add a tip on top of the service charge (although it's always welcome, of course). In some areas, such as Eastern Europe, tipping hasn't traditionally been an issue—but as this region becomes more of a tourism destination, tipping is becoming more expected there than it was previously. One appropriate rule of thumb is that if you're in a Western-style hotel, tipping is more likely to be expected, even if the traditional local culture wouldn't expect it.

Even within geographical areas such as the Middle East, Asia, and Africa, tipping practices vary widely. In Japan, for example, it's not expected. If you receive outstanding service that you believe should be rewarded, however, the appropriate way to present the money—which is considered a gift, rather than a tip—is in an envelope. It doesn't have to be a special envelope—a plain white one will do—and it can be marked with a simple "thank you."

You might think that tipping would be expected in Australia and New Zealand, but it's not so. Most restaurant servers don't expect tips, and taxi drivers are happy if you simply take the fare to the next full dollar.

As I said, it's important to check out standard practices at your destination before you get there. You'll know whether or not you need to have those small bills handy, you'll avoid the risk of offending the people you encounter along the way, and you'll feel much more relaxed and confident that you're doing the right thing. One of the best ways to judge a traveller is by the way they treat people they'll likely never meet again. It brings our world together in a better way if we treat everyone well, and tipping is part of that.

Cultural Sensitivities

Part of the wonder of travel is the opportunity to meet people from other cultures, and to gain insight into those cultures. This can be a bit tricky, however, because we don't always know how those cultures tend to speak, dress, manage personal space, or even handle disagreements. In Thailand, for example, it's considered extremely bad form to say anything negative about the country's monarchy. Again, researching your destination ahead of time will give you the best guide to any problems that may arise because of cultural differences.

MAKING A FIRST IMPRESSION: CLOTHING

From the comfy walking shoes on your feet to the sun-protecting hat on your head, dressing for comfort needs to be a priority when you're travelling. If your heels end up with blisters or your scalp gets sunburned, you could spend the rest of your vacation in pain, which wouldn't be much fun at all. But you also need to consider the impression that your clothes make.

If we're escaping a cold winter, we're often tempted to dress for the warmth of our destination. But before you throw your inhibitions out the window and strip down to the bare minimum, you need to take some time to consider your destination, and how the local people tend to dress.

For example, in many all-inclusive resorts, it's probably fine to walk around the pool and beach area in a swimsuit and light cover-up. But in the restaurant areas and outside the resort, clothing standards are likely more modest. In some countries, that may not matter too much, but in others, it could be a serious breach of etiquette. The last thing you want to do is offend someone in whose country you're a guest, or set yourself up as a target for rude remarks or behaviour. In Egypt, for example, dressing in skimpy clothes to walk around the streets and stores will likely attract stares and possibly remarks from passersby, particularly men. And even in North America, many stores and restaurants have a "no shoes, no shirt, no service" policy.

It's better to respect local customs, and dress relatively modestly, despite the heat. You'll gain more respect in return, and will likely find that you're treated better. Dressing appropriately includes wearing items that are in good repair, by the way. In some places, tattered jeans or T-shirts that have seen better days will be interpreted as being disrespectful to the local culture.

This crosses over into other issues in countries where women in particular are expected to dress very conservatively. Some people feel that this is an issue of principle and that they're standing up for their rights as human beings to dress in the way that they prefer. However, you have to remember that not respecting someone else's culture when you're in their country could be very insulting to them. Remember that you have chosen to visit that country in full knowledge (I hope) of their customs and traditions, and you should adhere to their standards for the duration of your stay.

Travel Best Bet!

Friends who travel frequently to warm climates suggest buying a couple of inexpensive outfits worn by the local people as a way to stay cool (the clothing is often lightweight) and appropriate. And if you're visiting any kind of religious building, from a cathedral to a mosque, be prepared: shorts (for men and for women) and halter tops will most probably not be appropriate. Choose pants or skirts, and shirts that have shoulders rather than straps. It's also a good idea for women to tuck a lightweight scarf into their purse or pack, as staff in some religious buildings will ask women to cover their heads. You should also consider wearing slip-on (rather than lace-up) shoes, which can be handy for places that ask you to remove your shoes.

PANHANDLERS AND AGGRESSIVE STREET SALESPEOPLE

It's not unusual to encounter panhandlers and aggressive street salespeople in many areas, and they're not restricted to developing or poorer countries. Depending on where you are in the world, they may be part of well-organized and semi-professional gangs that have created a business out of sending their most pitiful-looking children onto the streets in the hopes that people—especially tourists—will feel sorry or guilty enough to give them money.

It's important to remember that the child you give money to may be collecting it on behalf of one of these gangs. If you feel truly moved about the plight of the local people, I often suggest finding a reputable and legitimate non-profit organization that's working in the area and perhaps making a donation to them.

Whether it's a panhandler or salesperson who's approaching you and asking (or demanding) that you give them money or look at their goods, your strategy should be the same: keep walking and tell them a firm "no, thank you" in their own language. Don't engage in conversation or debate, don't get angry, and don't physically push them away. Simply avoid eye contact if you can, and be firm but pleasant about saying no or walking away. At the same time, stay alert as to where you are, and where your valuables are. Sometimes panhandlers or salespeople may be trying to distract you while someone else lifts your wallet out of your purse or pocket.

If you're in an area that's known for its challenging street life, ask your hotel concierge or front desk staff what the best approach is. Some countries and cities employ "tourist police" whose job is to keep an eye out for tourists and make sure that they're not being hassled too much. It's not a bad idea to do your shopping or strolling in the areas where they patrol.

THAT'S NOT WHAT I MEANT!

It isn't only words that can be a barrier when you're travelling. Gestures, personal space, and even acceptable topics of conversation differ between various cultures. To avoid giving offence, it's important to understand what's okay—and not okay—in the countries you'll be visiting. Here are a few examples to get you started.

- If you put your hands on your hips in Mexico, it could be considered a sign of hostility.

- In many Muslim countries, it's very important to remove your shoes when entering a home or mosque, and to avoid using your left hand for functions such as eating.

- In many Buddhist countries, it's considered rude or offensive to pat someone on their head, or to expose the sole of your shoe in someone's direction.

- In Italy, the sign we know as "okay" (thumb and finger forming a circle) is considered very rude.

- In many Asian countries, such as China and Japan, people tend to stand much closer to each other than in North America, especially on public transportation.

Calling Home

It's never been easier to stay in touch with friends, family, and the office while you're away from home. Whether you actually want to stay in touch with the office is, of course, another matter, but it is possible! The best and cheapest way to communicate is via e-mail. A free account such as Yahoo, Hotmail, or Google can be accessed from any computer with Internet access, and you'll find plenty of these in hotels or Internet cafés almost everywhere you go.

If you're travelling with a laptop, notebook, or PDA that connects to the Internet, either through cables or wirelessly, it's even easier. Just find a place to connect, and you're there. But you really don't need to take computer equipment on the road with you. Many hotels have business centres with computers, or you can check if there are Internet cafés or other sources of computer time nearby. Just be aware that hotels can charge a lot more for Internet connections than other places do, so always ask how much the charges are before you log on.

> ### Travel Best Bet!
> A friend who travelled through Italy recently discovered very inexpensive computer time at the public library in a small town. The time limit on the computer was only 20 minutes per person per day, but it was enough to check e-mail messages and deal with any urgent matters.

If you'd prefer to call home, be aware that it can be very expensive to do so, especially from the phone in your hotel room. When you check in, ask how much long distance calls cost per minute, and what (if any) surcharge the hotel will bill you for. Also find out if the hotel imposes surcharges even if you're using a calling card. It can be much cheaper to use a calling card at a payphone.

Of course, if you have a cellphone that works in the area that you're travelling in, that's a good option. Again, check out the rates before you leave. You'll be paying for long-distance charges and probably also for "roaming" charges. Some car rental agencies offer cellphone rental, too. That's a great option if your own cellphone won't work on the local network, but you should check with your cellphone provider about their service area. You may find your cellphone works—or doesn't work—in the most unexpected places.

Before you leave, look into calling cards that are often available through your telephone company and make sure that you call them using a network such as Canada Direct, which provides toll-free numbers in countries around the world. You simply call the number, tell the operator which company you're with (e.g., Bell or Telus), and they'll connect you right through to that company's operator/automated response system so that you can make the call you need. Canada Direct offers a small wallet-size card that lists the toll-free numbers you'll need. You can also find these at www.infocanadadirect.com.

On the road, you can buy pre-paid phone cards. When you purchase them, ask which phones they can be used in. It's best if they can be used at any phone but in some countries they may be restricted to phone services from certain companies.

Shop 'Til You Drop... or Not

You would think that shopping is nothing but fun, but it can be a little harrowing if you're expected to bargain or "haggle" with the salesperson or shopkeeper. Most of us are used to looking at the price tag, estimating the tax, and simply handing over the money. In many countries, however—especially in the markets —you'll be expected to come back with a price of your own. There's a real art to this and it can seem quite intimidating at the beginning, but it can be a lot of fun once you know what you're doing.

First, find out whether bargaining is expected at your destination. Then, dress down slightly (wearing expensive jewellery while claiming that you can't afford a trinket's price is not the way to wear down the shopkeeper!). If you have time, shop around a little to find out what kinds of products are on sale and at what price. Fellow travellers can be a great help with this. Of course, if you only have a morning to shop, or you're travelling constantly, you'll need to take a chance and simply buy when you see something you like.

Make sure that you have the local currency (or US currency, if that's what local storekeepers prefer), and take plenty of small bills. It's a favourite ploy of storekeepers to claim that they can't make change for a larger bill. Also, keep your shopping money separate from your other money. It's not a good idea to reveal how much cash you're carrying, and if you're making the point later that this is all the money you have with you, you don't want your travel expense money mixed up with your shopping money.

Knowing a few phrases in the local language will help you a lot, as it starts the transaction out on a friendly footing. Numbers are often difficult to keep straight, however, so take a small calculator. If you're having trouble understanding or being understood, you can punch in the figures on the calculator and show them to the storekeeper. Good old pen and paper work well, too.

When you're ready to buy, take a good look at the item to make sure that it doesn't have any flaws. Even if you don't find any, avoid appearing too enthusiastic (think of this stage as if you're buying a car at home—you don't want to reveal too much to the salesperson!). Find things to dislike (make them up if you need to): the colour, the workmanship, the size, for example. Then suggest a figure well below the asking price (here's where your research can come in handy: if you know what the pieces usually go for, you can start your bargaining well below that price, and work your way up). The price suggestions will then go back and forth: the storekeeper will come down, and you'll come up. Keep the exchange light—the storekeeper may feign great offence and get quite loud, but remember that this is a game that plays out all day, every day. Smile, stay calm and relaxed, and enjoy it. If nothing else, you'll have a funny story to relate once you're back home.

Tactics that may gain you better value include offering to buy more than one of the items after you've started bargaining. For example, try "Well, if that's the price for one tablecloth how much would three be?" It can be to your advantage to do a lot of shopping in one shop or stall to take advantage of "bulk" prices.

If you're still unhappy with the price, shrug your shoulders and simply walk away. Most of the time, the storekeeper will try giving you one last price. If they don't, you may want to find a more receptive shop or stall.

HANDY SHOPPING TIPS

- Resist getting carried away by the lure of bargains. Ask yourself if you really need the item, whether you have room to take it home (especially given baggage weight restrictions), where it will go when you get it home, or whether your friends will appreciate this particular souvenir of a place they've never been to.

- Remember to factor in the exchange rate and any taxes or duties you'll have to pay on the way home.

- If you're feeling pressured by a salesperson, don't be afraid to walk away.

- Know what something is worth back home to make sure that you're really getting a good price (this is particularly true for higher-end items such as art and jewellery).

- Many hotels, cruise ships, and tourist associations will list local stores that they recommend. These may not be the least expensive places, but they'll usually give you a reasonable price without trying to take advantage of you.

- Recognize that it's going to be very difficult to obtain a refund. Make sure you're happy with the purchase, and check it carefully for flaws before you leave the store.

- It's generally safest and least expensive to carry the items home yourself rather than have them shipped. If you do opt to have them shipped, you need to factor in the cost and make sure that the shipment is insured in case of loss or damage.

- Keep an eye on your purchases as they're being packaged or put into a bag to make sure that you actually receive everything that you paid for.

- In many stalls and stores, credit cards may not be accepted. Where they are, make sure that you keep your card in sight at all times. Don't let the store-keeper disappear with it in case it's being swiped twice, for example, and check the receipt to make sure that the price on it is correct.

- Keep your wits about you, and let your common sense prevail.

STAYING OUT OF SHOPPING TROUBLE

Certain items are riskier than others to buy when you're travelling, including art, antiques, and, in some cases, local crafts. Many countries limit the age of items that you can take across their borders to protect antiquities. In other cases, trade of products made from certain animals, such as endangered species, is illegal. Make sure that you know the rules and stick to them. And remember that you usually can't take food items such as meat, dairy produce, fruit, or vegetables across international borders, so trying to take that delicious local cheese back home is **NOT** a good idea.

A TAXING SITUATION

Before you travel, check whether or not the country in which you'll be shopping has a tax-refund policy for visitors. If they do, you'll likely be able to ask for a tax refund when you buy products over a certain value, or when your purchases collectively add up to a minimum value. Sometimes the store handles the paperwork for you; at other times, you'll collect the paperwork at the store or airport and fill it out before you leave the country. Many countries have a kiosk or a dedicated mailbox for tax refunds at airport departure lounges. Depending on the country's system, you'll either receive an immediate refund or it will be forwarded by mail to your home several weeks (or even months) later. It's worth a little research and paperwork to save the tax, which can add up to 15 to 20 percent of your purchase depending on your location.

Travel Best Bet!
You can get a tax break up front at many department stores in the United States if you're Canadian. All you need to do is go to the Customer Service counter and show them proof that you live in Canada. They'll then give you a coupon or card that you can use for the day that will entitle you to a tax discount. The amount of the discount depends on the state you're visiting. On my last visit to New York City, I saved 11 percent off everything I bought at Bloomingdale's and Macy's.

We're Leaving When? Schedule Changes

Okay, so you've carefully planned your itinerary down to the last second but suddenly, out of the blue, you discover that your airline has changed the timing of your flight. Can they do that??

Yes, absolutely, they can—and so can tour operators, cruise lines, and other travel service providers. Despite what it says on your tickets, no departure is ever guaranteed to be on time or even on the same type of equipment (planes, for example, get switched all the time). This can happen for all sorts of reasons: everything from weather to mechanical issues to labour unrest. Usually your travel service provider will do the best they can to get you where you're going as quickly as possible, but delays still happen.

That's why I strongly suggest that when you're planning your trip, you never schedule a flight arrival just a few hours prior to a tour starting or a cruise ship departing. If you're delayed, that tour or ship is going to leave without you and you'll have missed part or all of your vacation. Unless you've booked your flight with a company that guarantees they'll "catch you up" to your tour or ship, you're also on the hook for the added expense. Even if the delay was caused by the carrier (for example, a mechanical problem with the aircraft), which may increase their responsibility for compensation, you'll still have missed part of your tour or cruise. It's best to arrive a day ahead of the scheduled departure, to give yourself that "just in case" room.

Although airlines and other travel providers will often ask you for a phone number where they can reach you in case of schedule changes, don't rely on being contacted. Always confirm your details within 24 hours of your expected departure. Airlines in particular often say that you don't need to confirm your seat, but look at it this way: you're not confirming your seat, you're confirming your departure. And if the airline does require confirmation within a certain time period, make sure that you follow their instructions closely, and call to make that confirmation (in both directions!). If you don't, they can give your seat to someone else, or fail to notify you of a schedule change.

Oh No! Lost Passports

If the worst happens and your passport is lost or stolen, you need to call your nearest consulate or embassy immediately. You'll likely have to go there in person to apply for a temporary or replacement passport. Make sure that you ask them what identification and other paperwork, photos, or fees you'll need to bring with you. If the passport was stolen, you may also need to report it to the local police and obtain a written report from them.

This is one of the biggest wrenches that can be thrown into your trip schedule. It's going to take time to travel to the consulate/embassy, and it's going to take time for your new passport to be issued, because they'll likely conduct an investigation into what happened (expect to be questioned closely about the loss) and they'll need time to process the paperwork.

Anything that you can do to make it easier for government officials will make the situation better. At the very least, you'll need your passport number. If you're carrying a photocopy of the passport, that's even better. You may also need some kind of proof of citizenship. Ask the officials what they'll accept, and—if necessary—have someone courier it from home.

If you're likely to be delayed beyond your planned return date, call your travel agent to see if they can do anything for you in terms of rescheduling your return or helping you book alternative hotels. If you're not working with an agent, call the airline and explain the situation to see if they can help. They may be able to change your flights, although there will likely be a fee involved. Also call your trip cancellation insurance provider (you did buy trip cancellation insurance, didn't you?), to let them know that you may need to make a claim, and to find out if there are any special procedures that you need to follow.

When you arrive back home, you should apply for a replacement passport. Expect it to take a little longer than usual, however, as there may be a follow-up investigation for lost or stolen passports.

CLAIRE'S BEST BETS FOR LOGISTICAL LOGIC

- Remember: Be Flexible, Organized, and Prepared—and calm!
- Do your research so you know what the local customs are, including tipping, clothing, and shopping.
- Always respect the culture of the country that you're visiting. You're the outsider, remember.
- Dissuade aggressive panhandlers or salespeople with a firm "no, thank you," preferably in their language if you can manage it.
- Plan to have fun shopping, but remember, it's always "buyer beware."
- Double-check your schedule so that you'll know if any changes have been made.
- If you lose your passport, start the replacement process (and some deep-breathing exercises) immediately.

Chapter 11
All in the Family: Travelling with Kids

Keeping It in the Family

Until you're a parent, you cannot possibly appreciate how much is involved in getting every member of the family ready to get out the door each morning, let alone for a family vacation. Family vacations take a lot of planning and preparation. I know this from experience. I also know that it's all worth it, because family vacations can provide some of the best memories of your life. This chapter contains some tips and advice to help you make your next family vacation memorable, more stress free, and above all, fun.

INVOLVE THE KIDS

Get the kids on board by involving them in the planning. Their specific role will depend on their age and your patience, but it could be colouring in a map of the route, reading books or watching movies about the destination, helping to find a hotel within a certain budget, and planning which attractions to visit. They can also participate in packing. Even small children can choose a favourite toy and book to pop in their suitcase (although it doesn't hurt for you to pop a few extras in your suitcase, especially if you suspect that your child has made a choice he or she will later regret).

 Travel Best Bet!
A friend's sister gave her five-year-old son his own disposable camera when they took a driving vacation through the Rocky Mountains. It gave him a lot of pleasure to be in charge of his own photos, and she said that although he didn't take the most traditional photos, some of them were downright artistic!

KEEP THEM BUSY

Books, toys, stickers, games, portable DVD and game players, books on tape, and music CDs to sing along with can all make a huge difference to how happy your child is while en route. You could even put together an activity bag for each child, perhaps keeping it as a surprise for when they get into the car or onto the plane. Once you're at your destination, find a way for them to blow off steam by playing active games or going for a walk on the beach. Physical activity is a great stress reliever for the whole family. (Try seat-bound yoga stretches in cars and planes!)

CARRY EXTRAS

Extra moistened wipes, extra changes of clothes, extra snacks (buy extra drinks once you're through airport security if you're flying, because security rules restrict the amount of liquids you can bring in carry-on luggage), extra toys and books, and extra bottles or pacifiers. Expect that extra plastic, recloseable freezer bags will become your new best friends.

MAKE LISTS—AND CHECK THEM TWICE

Okay, so you may be able to "grab and go" for yourself at the last minute, but don't try this with kids. You may not mind if you forget your favourite tooth-brush, but if you forget theirs, you'll never hear the end of it. With apologies to Santa for stealing his strategy, make a list for each child and check it twice. Then have the children collect everything on their own list (if practical), and check off the items with you. That way you'll have a better shot at nice, instead of naughty.

ADAPT YOUR SCHEDULE TO THEIRS

You may be used to planning a trip based on how long you're willing to sit in a car, or what time of day you prefer to fly. Welcome to a brave, new world! To reduce the likelihood of toddler and small child temper explosions, travel on their schedule instead; specifically, their sleep schedule. A long flight or car journey will be so much easier if you can do it while they're sleeping—usually overnight. You'll have to factor in the fact that you'll be arriving at the destination exhausted, while the kids will be refreshed and ready to go, but it may be your best option for a quiet flight or drive. Plan for plenty of bathroom breaks or diaper changes, too.

KNOW WHEN TO FOLD 'EM

Vacations BC (before children) may have involved art galleries, sculpture museums, and historic monuments. Vacations AC (you get the idea) can involve those only in small doses, unless you're looking for an active rebellion. Vacations will be happier for everyone involved if they're geared to activities that your children will enjoy and can fully participate in, and if they include some "downtime" for the children when they can play independently or read.

Travel Best Bet!
Want to know where the best washrooms are (or even where ANY washrooms are) at your sightseeing destinations? Check them ahead of time at www.thebathroom diaries.com. And for best results, always carry your own toilet paper and hand sanitizer gel, just in case.

DON'T FORGET PARENT STRESS RELIEVERS

And no, I don't mean tranquilizers. Recognize that you need adult time on your vacation, too. If it's practical, plan on taking advantage of children's programs and babysitting at resorts and hotels and on cruises. Perhaps arrange with your partner to give each other a couple of hours of "alone" time when you need it most. Pack individual sachets of bubble bath just for you once everyone's tucked into bed.

THINK HEALTHY

Everyone's going to be in a better mood if you can moderate sugar intake, keep kids and adults well hydrated (despite the resulting bathroom breaks!), and avoid hunger pangs. Smaller meals or snacks eaten at frequent intervals can work really well. You may have to restrict fruit and veggies if you're flying internationally, but otherwise, snack-size portions are a fantastic idea for journeys, as are crackers, cheese, and basically anything that's not packed with sugar. Save sugary snacks for an occasional treat when nerves are on the ropes. (Don't forget something for yourself!)

EMERGENCIES 'R US

Go through your medical supplies at home, and think about what you'd do if your child said they had a headache, stuffy nose, or tummy ache, if they fell down and hurt themselves, or if they started running a fever. Whatever you need in response to common childhood ailments, bring it along. While you may be able to find supplies at your destination, it will be less than convenient, and possibly not even an option, to run out to the nearest drugstore in the middle of the night.

Before You Leave Home

Before you load the car and lock the door, take care of the following details—your journey will be much smoother if you do.

PUT THE PAPERWORK TOGETHER

Months before your departure date, make sure that all the kids have an up-to-date passport if you're travelling across the border. Even babies now need their own passport. The days of being added to a parent's passport are long gone. And even if you're not heading out of the country, it's still a good idea to have some kind of identification for each child.

It's also absolutely essential that you have the proper documentation to prove that each child is with you legally. This is critical if you're travelling across international borders, but I recommend it even if you're travelling within them. If, for example, you're taking one of your children's friends on a family ski trip, or if you're not travelling with your own child's other parent, having a notarized letter of consent from the other parent(s) involved can prove instantly that you have permission to travel with the child. This letter is an absolute requirement for international travel, but it can avoid a lot of problems even domestically, too. (See also "Paperwork: Beyond the Red Tape" in Chapter 1, Planning for Paradise.)

PLAN FOR DISASTER

No one ever wants to think about their children becoming lost from the main family group when they're travelling, but it does happen, even to the best of parents and children. Talk about a panic factor! Obviously, you're going to do everything that you can to prevent this, but a little preparation can really help, just in case.

Talk to your child in an age-appropriate way about what to do if they get separated from you, and reinforce that message on every day of the trip. Each child should carry their own identification, including your cellphone number, to enable them or the authorities to contact you right away. If it's at all practical, having a cellphone for each member of the family can be a huge help in these situations.

Before you leave, make sure that you have an up-to-date photograph of each child who's travelling with you, and their vital statistics, including height, weight, blood type, any allergies, and the contact information for their doctor(s) back home.

PACK FOR EVERYONE

Although it's a great idea to have your children pack their own bags, at least as far as their age and enthusiasm allow, you're still the parent. Double-check that they have everything they need. It's a good idea to restrict their hand luggage, even if you're not flying—otherwise you tend to end up loaded down with their bags, too.

Depending on the age of your children, it's probably best for you to carry any medications that may be needed. You'll be the best judge of who should carry what, of course, but if you're flying, make sure that the medication is packed in carry-on bags and that the child's name on the medication's label matches the name on their ticket.

Travel Best Bet!
A good friend of mine told me that she wouldn't go on a vacation because she found it easier to be home with the baby swing, high chair, full-size stroller, etc. The thought of not having those items while on vacation made her not want to go on one at all. What she didn't know is that at many destinations you can rent those necessary baby items. They have everything! The rental company will bring the items to your hotel or condo the day you arrive, and pick them up the day you leave. It's a great way to make travelling with young children easier!

Teenage Trials and Tribulations

Teenagers require special handling at the best of times. Travelling with them can be a wonderful bonding experience for everyone, but it's definitely not for the faint of heart. The best way to get them on board—physically and emotionally—is to have them help you plan the trip. If they can choose some of the attractions and activities for the family, or if they can participate in some of them on their own (in a controlled setting, of course, such as in a hotel or cruise ship youth program), they'll probably be a lot more accepting of the upheaval that a trip will create.

You also need to work within their schedule to a certain extent. Teenagers are well known for staying up late and sleeping late. Make a deal with them that you're not going to roust them out of bed super-early, but that you expect them to be ready to go at a mutually agreed-upon time. Of course, there's no reason why you can't go out and get your day started, and return for them later!

You know your teen best, especially when it comes to being sociable. If you're concerned that they may not be able to make friends along the way, or that they'll feel a little "on their own" (for example, if they're an only child), consider suggesting that they ask a friend to come with them. You'll likely be paying for many of the friend's expenses, but it could be worth it to keep everyone happy. Be prepared for the odd moment of tension between friends, though, as they won't be used to be spending quite so much time together.

In the same vein, consider what keeps them happy at home—whether it's reading, listening to music, or playing electronic games—and, arrange for them to bring it with them. Remember to pack spare batteries for any gadgets you bring.

What goes for smaller children can also apply to teens: build in plenty of breaks and downtime, don't let them get too hungry, have them pack their own bags, and involve them in the journey, whether it's asking questions about local history or having them monitor your position on the map.

Sky High: Flying with Children

It's a great idea to talk to your children ahead of time if they've never flown before. Let them know what to expect. To build anticipation (although you probably won't have to), you can even take them to the airport on a special family field trip to let them watch the planes take off and land. If you sense that your child has any anxiety about the trip, talk it through with them.

While you're building their anticipation, make sure you also book early and request seats together. Families are often assigned to the rows in front of the bulkhead because there's slightly more room there, plus hooks for a baby bassinet that the flight attendants can mount to give your arms a break if you're travelling with an infant. You can't use the bassinet during take-off and landing, or during in-flight turbulence, but it can be a huge bonus during a long flight.

On most flights, a child who's under two years old can travel on your lap either free of charge or for a nominal fare. However, for extra safety (and your own comfort) you may want to consider booking them their own seat, and bringing their car seat with you. The US Federal Aviation Administration (www.faa.gov) strongly recommends that children who weigh less than 40 pounds (18.1 kilos) use a child restraint system. This could be a car seat or a CARES system (see below). It may be a little more awkward to travel with, but it's all about safety.

It's best to seat children in the middle of a row or next to a window if you can. If they're in an aisle seat they run the risk of interfering with, or being bumped by, people or equipment that's passing by. A middle seat is a better bet, particularly if they have a parent on either side of them. A window seat is best if you're travelling on your own with them, though—they're less likely to annoy a passenger who would otherwise be seated next to them.

Travel Best Bet!

*A device named CARES—short for Child Aviation Restraint System—is a great investment if you plan on travelling a lot with young children. It's a harness-like tool that connects to an airplane seat belt and fits around the back of the seat, with straps that go over toddlers' shoulders to hold them in case of heavy turbulence or a crash. It's intended for kids who are 12 months and older, and who weigh between 22 and 44 pounds (10 and 20 kilos). The harness itself weighs just 1 pound, so it's a **LOT** lighter than hauling a car seat with you onto the plane, and it installs in one minute (super fast!). It's the first of its kind to be approved for use on all commercial airlines, and is well worth looking at. CARES costs about US$75, and is available at www.kidsflysafe.com.*

Take-offs and landings can be uncomfortable for anyone's ears, but they can be especially tough on babies and small children. Having young children suck on a bottle or juice box will help them swallow to help equalize the pressure; older children can try chewing gum or a piece of hard candy; and for babies, a pacifier can be comforting.

Travel Best Bet!

Shortly after we boarded a plane to Palm Springs when my son was two years old, my husband was horrified to find him licking the arm rest. Luckily, I knew my toddler very well and had wiped down our entire section—arm rests, windows, and trays—before the licking took place. My husband was both surprised and relieved that I had thought ahead about this. You know your own children best, so do what you need to do to keep them safe and healthy—no matter how it may look to other people!

You'll have to push your mind-reading powers to their limit to ensure you bring on board everything that your children will need. The longer the trip, the more stamina and imagination you may need to keep them happy and occupied. Inevitably, however, there will come a point where they're not happy, which means no one around them is happy. You know them best. Do whatever you can to distract them or mollify them. I know it's really difficult to remain unfrazzled yourself when this happens—I've been there, and you can actually feel the eyes of the passengers around you rolling—but keep in mind that, in reality, most of them are parents, and deep down most of them understand. Your best chance at reducing your child's stress levels is not to increase your own, because they can sense when you're tense.

Travelling with Babies and Toddlers

Travelling with children is one thing; travelling with babies and toddlers is a whole other challenge. One of the biggest logistical issues is, of course, diaper changing. Location isn't usually a problem: even on aircraft there's usually at least one washroom with a fold-down change table. When it comes to potty training, however, I don't have any easy answers. Whether you're on a plane or in a vehicle, quick access to a washroom may not be an option. I'd suggest planning around it instead, perhaps even leaving it for when you return from a trip if you can.

Feeding is a little bit easier to work around. The disposable bottle liners that are pre-sterilized in a roll are excellent for long journeys. Carry a bottle of pre-boiled water with you too (if you're flying, check whether security regulations allow you to carry it through in your hand luggage), then make up the bottle in the pre-sterilized bag. If you're flying, you can ask the attendant to warm the bottle by standing it briefly in a bowl of hot water. Restaurant staff will also do this for you. I recommend that people travelling with babies also travel with a little plug-in kettle. You'll be able to sterilize bottles, sippy cups, and dishes using the boiling water. The boiled water can also be bottled and used later to add to formula, infant cereal, etc.

For privacy (good for nursing!) and shade from the sun, try keeping two diaper pins attached to your diaper bag. You can pin a blanket to your seat and the seat in front of you for a privacy screen.

Always carry a change of clothes for your child, and a change of top/T-shirt for yourself, too—you never know when you'll need it. Disposable bibs are a great idea for infant mealtimes when you're on the road.

I always found an infant front pack—my favourite was a BabyBjörn—to be a great option, because I could carry my baby while pushing a luggage cart or pulling a suitcase. Small travel strollers are also a good option (they'll fit in the luggage bins of 747s or larger aircraft, but airlines have become increasingly strict about not allowing these on board so check with the airline first).

If you're flying, only choose bulkhead seats if your baby needs a baby bassinet. If not, take any other seats in preference. On the bulkhead seats the armrest can't be moved, while on normal seats the armrests can go up. The latter option is far better if your baby wants to lie down on the seat with her head on your lap.

Surviving a Car Trip

Fear not: you can survive a car trip with kids, although I'll admit that it can be a little trying at times. A friend of mine who is quite experienced at driving the massive six-lanes-in-one-direction M25 motorway, the orbital route around London, England, told me that it added a whole new degree of difficulty when she found herself with a very unhappy and jet-lagged two-year-old in the back seat. Oh, those wonderful toddler days! (Not to mention the equally outstanding teething times.)

This is when road games (how many times can you play I Spy?), DVDs, music CDs, and electronic games can be absolute sanity savers. The best—and possibly safest—strategy, though, is to travel during nap time or regular sleep time, and to plan plenty of breaks.

Travel Best Bet!

Many of my clients take their own children's car seats with them when they're renting a vehicle, even if the rental agency has car seats available. The car seats may be bulky and awkward to travel with, but they're like a miniature familiar world for your child and they're likely to be more comfortable than rental car seats, too. Plus, they're a known factor in terms of meeting safety requirements. Before you hit the road, double-check that all the car seat buckles and straps are properly fastened.

Along with the items I mentioned at the beginning of the chapter, pack some extra garbage bags and paper towels in case of spills in the car. Speaking of spills, there's no avoiding the topic of motion sickness, the bane of many a parent. If it's an issue, talk to your doctor ahead of time about medications or techniques that can help. Asking your child to look at the horizon can help: avoid having them read or watch DVDs in the car if motion sickness is an issue. It may also be wise to limit certain types of food and drink before and during the trip, such as treats or meals with high sugar or fat contents.

Going It Alone: Single-Parent Travel

Whether you're a full-time single parent or simply travelling alone with the kids while your partner is otherwise occupied, travelling on your own with kids can be a wonderful, rewarding, hair-raising, and nerve-wracking experience. Yes, all at the same time!

Your first challenge is to find a reasonably priced vacation option, especially if you're not fond of the usual budget-boosting options such as camping. Since most hotel prices are based on double occupancy, you may find it best to share a room with your children to avoid paying the single supplement, assuming that you can get separate beds and possibly a pull-out couch or cot, if necessary. Only you can judge whether such a situation will work out well, based on your family dynamics and your children's ages.

You can also look at suite options. It can sometimes be cheaper to book a two-bedroom suite than two separate rooms. Vacation rentals such as apartments, condos, or houses also work well for families, but be aware that they may have minimum rental lengths, such as two nights over weekends or by the week, especially during peak season.

One increasingly viable option is to choose a trip designed specifically for single parents travelling with their children. I've seen several Mexican and Caribbean resorts offering all-inclusive vacations that waive the single supplement and even host an adults-only cocktail party for the parents, sometimes even providing baby-sitting. Some cruise ships are also marketing departures aimed at single parents.

Flying Solo: Children Travelling Alone

Although many major airlines permit children five and older to travel on their own, only you can judge whether they're mature enough to handle a solo journey with its unfamiliar surroundings and new situations to deal with. Keep in mind that many airlines now restrict solo children flyers to direct flights, so you'll need to book well ahead to make sure that you can get them seats on these flights. Many airlines also charge a fee for children travelling alone.

If you feel that your child is ready for a solo flight—perhaps to see a parent or grandparent, or to participate in a youth group such as a Boy Scout Jamboree —talk to them to make sure that they agree with you. Especially if they've never flown before, discuss what it will be like at the airports and on the plane. If you think it will help, write down some tips for them to carry with them. They should also carry identification, phone numbers to call in case of a flight cancellation or other emergency, and a way to make those calls (a calling card or a cellphone, for example).

Be sure that you emphasize to booking agents and check-in staff that your child is travelling alone. It was once standard to allow you through security and into the gate to wait with your child, but in today's security climate that can no longer be guaranteed. Be sure that you know the airline's policy so that you're clear on how your child will be escorted through security and to the gate, whether they'll be left alone to wait at the gate, if someone will be watching for them to board the plane, and how they'll be met at the arrival gate and taken through to collect their luggage.

Ask the check-in staff to seat your child next to a vacant seat if possible. This may not be practical in the case of a full plane, but it can help your child feel more comfortable. Make sure that your child knows they should talk to a flight attendant immediately if they're not feeling well, they're scared, or someone is making them feel uncomfortable for any reason. All these actions should help both of you feel a lot better about the flight.

CLAIRE'S BEST BETS FOR TRAVELLING WITH KIDS

- Involve your children as much as possible in the planning of your family travel, in an age-appropriate way. Include them in destination and route planning, packing, budgeting, and activity scheduling, as appropriate.

- Plan your itinerary around their schedule. Include lots of bathroom, snack, and play breaks, and travel when they're usually sleeping for a quieter trip.

- Make sure that every child has their own identification, including a passport if you're travelling internationally.

- Obtain a notarized letter of consent from the children's other guardians or parents, especially if you're travelling across borders.

- The FAA strongly recommends that children who weigh less than 40 pounds (18 kilos) use a child restraint system on aircraft.

- Bring everything with you that you and your children will need— medication, snacks, books, and toys—to keep you relaxed and them busy and happy.

- Only consider letting your child travel alone if you're absolutely sure they can handle the experience.

- Put your children's needs first when you travel together to keep them—and you—happy.

Chapter 12
Specialty Travel

Theme Park Thrills

If you're taking the family for a theme park vacation, you want the roller coaster rides to be inside the park and not part of the vacation itself. Choosing the right theme park, one that will keep all ages of the family happy, can help. Check them out online, send for their brochures (and even promotional videos or DVDs), and talk to a travel agent who is well versed in family and theme-park vacations. Many family-oriented websites will have travel reviews posted on them, so you can hear what real visitors have to say about the park.

Once you've found a theme park, you need to decide where to stay. It can certainly be convenient to find a hotel right at the theme park, and it may not be as expensive as you'd expect. Package deals that include accommodation and park entrance can make this much more affordable. However, there are usually plenty of accommodation options near major theme parks, and many of them offer free shuttles back and forth, thus eliminating parking issues and making it convenient for the family to split up at any point, with some returning to the hotel and others staying on at the park.

To obtain the best possible value, consider travelling at an off-peak time. If it's practical and possible, pull the kids out of school for a few days. You'll also find the park's rides and restaurants a little less crowded, taking away some of the potential stress that always hovers in the background when children are excited and impatient. However, it's always a good idea to talk to the school, as well as your children's teachers, first about their policy on taking children out during term time, especially if your children are older or their school operates on a semester system. It may be better from the school's point of view if you time your vacation for the end of the school year when things are winding down, rather than at the beginning of a new year when there is a greater focus on helping children—especially younger children—settle in to their new routine. (And try not to make a habit of pulling them out for an off-peak vacation!)

Once you've booked, have fun planning your park priorities. Research the rides and attractions as a family, and find out what everyone wants to see and do. Then come up with an itinerary. You can keep it as detailed or loose as you wish. It doesn't need to be set in stone once you've drawn it up but it gives you a place to begin. One of the biggest issues with theme parks is that they can feel quite overwhelming once you're inside them. Being able to fall back on your plan can minimize this, and it ensures that no member of the family will be left out.

If it's age appropriate, include a plan to split up once you're inside the park. Find a meeting place that everyone agrees on and a time to meet. Take cell-phones, just in case something comes up that changes your plans, as well as small snacks and bottled water. The cost of these can start to add up unexpectedly quickly if you buy them in the park.

> **TBB** *Travel Best Bet!*
> *On our last family vacation to Disneyland we took walkie-talkies with us (the same ones I took on the cruise). They were good quality and had a decent range. In fact, we could communicate when one person was in the hotel (across the street from the park) and the other was inside the park. They were so handy. I totally recommend them as a cheap and easy way to stay in touch.*

Even on busy days there are ways to beat the crowds. The busiest time is usually between noon and 4 p.m. so I recommend getting an early start. Arrive as soon as the park opens, or even just a little before. You could also head straight to the rides that are farthest away from the entrance to beat many other visitors who will gravitate to the rides nearest the entrance first.

I also think that taking a break "off-site" during the afternoon (the busiest time) before coming back in the late afternoon or evening is a good way to make the most of your day. A break at midday also gives you a chance to have a meal outside the park (where it will likely be less expensive), lets young children take a nap, and lets older children enjoy some pool time. If you don't have a multi-day pass, make sure that you find out about re-entry to the park. You'll often need to have your hand stamped. Remember, too, that this is your vacation, and it's supposed to be fun. If you're getting tired, take a break.

When the Honeymoon's Just Beginning

After the busy days before and during a wedding celebration, the honeymoon is all about enjoying a wonderful start to a new life. As far as destinations go, there are some perennial favourites for couples marrying in North America: Hawaii,

Mexico, and the Caribbean, for example. From Europe, many couples choose the Mediterranean or even the South Seas. The current trend seems to be to choose a cruise or a stay at an all-inclusive resort, both of which are certainly low-stress options. Not surprisingly, spa services are also a big seller when it comes to honeymoons.

I've also seen a growing trend to postpone the honeymoon. For example, some couples in Vancouver, BC, are choosing to spend a few nights away close to home, in Whistler or Victoria perhaps, and then book a longer vacation when it's more convenient for them to travel, when prices offer better value or the weather is a better bet, or simply when their budgets have recovered from the shock of the wedding itself.

It's important to decide together where you want to go, and how much you can afford to spend. A wedding can be a time of major expenses, and you don't want your honeymoon to end up putting you into so much debt that you spend your entire vacation worrying about how you're going to pay it off. If there's anything that you really want to include, though, put it on your list—maybe a private balcony on a cruise ship, or a resort with tons of fun activities to try. Choose your priorities, and then find a honeymoon that fulfills them. The perfect honeymoon is whatever you want to do, whether it's backpacking in the Rockies, island hopping in the South Pacific, or staying in a hotel across town. Some couples are even putting contributions to their honeymoon on their gift registry. It could be the perfect gift for the couple that already has a toaster!

You also need to decide when to leave. Many couples prefer to spend their first night at a hotel in their hometown so that they can stay at their wedding reception as long as they want to. Others remain nearby even longer so that they have more time to enjoy friends and family who have travelled in for the wedding.

When you're planning your honeymoon, let everyone that you're working with know that it's a special trip, and let people know along the way, too. Everyone loves a lover, and they also love to spoil you with bonuses and upgrades.

Travel Best Bet!
A television viewer from Vancouver wrote to me to ask an excellent question: should she book her honeymoon in her married name or her maiden name? She was right to check, because it's best to book under your maiden name. It can take quite a while to change your paperwork to your new name, and if the name on the airline ticket doesn't match the name on your identification, you won't be going anywhere.

DESTINATION WEDDINGS

Over the past several years I have noticed more and more couples choosing to have the whole wedding at a vacation destination, combining the honeymoon with the big day. Whether or not you invite friends and family, and how many, is completely up to you but keep in mind that your guest list constitutes a "group." That means your travel agent may be able to obtain some special rates or discounts for you. (See "Group Vacations: When Three's Not a Crowd" in Chapter 1, Planning for Paradise.)

It's essential to do your homework to find out what's required, both at your destination and in your local area, for you to be legally married when you return. Many resorts and visitors bureaus in warm-weather destinations have websites and brochures dedicated to destination weddings, so that will help. In fact, you can now hand the entire event over to many hotels and resorts. Simply tell them what you want and when you want it, and they'll take care of all the details.

Travel in Good Company: Guided Tours

Many people prefer not to organize their own travel. Their idea of holiday heaven is letting someone else take care of all the details, from reserving accommodations to driving them between attractions. That's where guided tour companies come in, and there's a stunning range to choose from. Your best bet for picking a tour that's a good fit is to start with three key factors: budget, age, and activity level.

Tour companies range from budget to luxury and everywhere in between. Some also cater to different age groups: the under-35s, baby boomers, and seniors, for example. Still others differentiate themselves based on what they offer. Walking holidays, historic tours, and wildlife watching are just a few of the offerings out there.

Research the tour company by reading its brochures and checking out its website. Both of these will give you a sense of the company's personality and target audience, which will help you decide if it's the right company for you. Most tour costs will be "land-only," meaning that you'll need to add on the cost of the airfare to get you from home to where the tour starts and back again. It's crucial to read all the fine print so that you clearly understand what's included on the tour and what's not. Also pay attention to how much "free time" you'll have. Many companies are now building this into their itineraries as they recognize that it's a good way to keep everyone on the trip happy.

Make absolutely sure that you're working with a reputable tour company. You should ask questions about their background, including how long they've been in business, how they researched the trip's itinerary, what training their guides have, whether they're registered with any consumer protection organizations, and what happens to your deposit if the company can't provide the trip for any reason.

Paying with a credit card may help if the trip is cancelled and you don't receive a refund, but when it comes to problems, it's more likely to be a situation where all is not as promised. Accommodation may not be up to standard, for example, or the itinerary may have been changed without prior notice. Dealing with a reputable company will minimize the chances of it happening, but if a problem does occur, you need to phone the company's main office immediately to try to get it sorted out. If that doesn't help, document the problems fully (take photos if applicable), and write to the company after you return home. Also write to any consumer protection agencies in your jurisdiction, and contact your credit card company to let them know that there's an amount in dispute if you haven't yet paid for the trip.

Lifelong Learning

Many travellers today aren't satisfied with the idea of lazing about on a beach. There's absolutely nothing wrong with either lazing about or beaches, of course, but there are also tons of opportunities to put your vacation to good use by learning something new. Whether it's brushing up on your Italian cooking skills at a culinary school in Tuscany or discovering how beluga whales communicate in Hudson Bay, there's bound to be a learning opportunity to match your interests.

Although various tour companies cater to learning adventures—one Canadian-based operation, www.routestolearning.ca, offers trips to many areas of the world, and caters to all ages and families—think a little outside the box, too. Many colleges and universities offer travel-study programs as part of their continuing education programs. Museums and zoos have also caught on to this trend—and who better to travel to Africa with than a zookeeper who specializes in lions and tigers (oh my)?

Travel Best Bet!

Have you ever wondered what goes on in the kitchen of a first-class resort? A friend spent a day learning the ropes as a commis or apprentice chef at the Four Seasons Resort Scottsdale at Troon North, in Arizona, and reported back that the executive chef didn't shout at anyone once. She peeled citrus fruit, chopped asparagus, loaded twice-baked potatoes with their fillings, and thoroughly enjoyed herself, all while learning new kitchen skills and feasting on a stellar meal at the end of the day.

Adventure Travel

Adventure travel has been growing steadily in popularity since the early 1990s. It gives you the chance to see the world by going off the beaten track, to the heart of the destination, and meeting the local people. Many companies offer small group tours led by professional guides who share their experience and knowledge of a destination along the way.

No matter what you are looking for—from trekking in Nepal to kayaking in the Baja, cycling through France or exploring Machu Picchu—rest assured that there will be a company that offers it. And you don't have to be 25 years old or run marathons to go on an adventure holiday. Adventure trips are available for all ages and fitness levels. All you need is a curiosity for culture and the desire to explore an area in more detail. Many say that once you've been on an adventure travel trip you're hooked for life!

 The two websites I recommend most to those looking for adventure travel are www.gapadventures.com and www.adventures-abroad.com.

Volunteer Vacations

You may prefer to give something back as part of your vacation. If you're an active traveller, love to learn about the local culture, and have a passion for contributing to the planet on which we all live, a volunteer vacation may be just the ticket for you. Solo travellers often find that it's a great way to vacation—they can meet fun people with similar interests while doing something that feels worthwhile.

In most cases, the volunteers pay their own travel costs, including airfare and accommodation, which may be quite basic. Sometimes the trip's cost includes a donation; sometimes it doesn't. Volunteers with some organizations may also be asked to find sponsors for their trip or project. Much of this depends on the particular organization that you'd like to work with.

So what could you find yourself doing? Perhaps building a house or school, digging wells for water, teaching English as a second language, helping to set up micro-businesses, clearing trails in national parks, or monitoring wildlife numbers. No matter what your skills or interests are, there's sure to be a volunteer vacation that will suit you.

A travel agent or an Internet search may be a great source of volunteer vacation choices, or talk to your favourite local charitable or non-profit organization to see if they're linked to a vacation network. Wherever you choose to contribute, just be sure to do your homework so that you understand exactly what's required of you in terms of both costs and work. This is especially important for health and safety concerns, such as vaccinations (see Chapter 4, Staying Healthy, and Chapter 5, Staying Safe). Always read the fine print!

Girls' Getaways and "Man-cations"

It's a fact of life that many couples simply don't want to go to the same places or do the same things when they're on vacation. Plus, there are plenty of single women and men out there who don't necessarily want to travel solo, but aren't interested in a "singles" trip either.

Enter the girls' getaway, which has recently been joined by the "man-cation." The trips bring the sexes together (separately!) for a relaxed trip that's focused entirely on what they want to do. Popular girls' getaways include spa weekends, pyjama parties hosted by major hotels, mother-daughter trips, special occasion celebrations, and adventure trips where the women feel they can learn new skills or try new activities in a very supportive atmosphere. The boys' getaways tend to be action-oriented, focused on a sporting event, adventure trip, or a special occasion celebration.

While some of these trips, such as the hotel pyjama parties, involve pre-planned package deals, keep in mind when you're planning a trip like this that you may qualify as a group, and thus be eligible for discounts or bonuses on some of your travel expenses. You don't need to be part of a group to attend these events, however—many welcome single travellers to join in the fun.

Accessible Travel

The logistics of travel can be challenging for everyone. Add a disability to the mix and it can become even more so. The good news is that many transport and tour companies, attractions, and accommodations are making travel for those with disabilities much easier by making their sites more accessible. In some countries, this is mandated by the government; in others, companies have realized that it's simply good for business. This is where research becomes imperative if you want to make sure that your vacation is as stress-free and easy to navigate as possible.

For example, the Underground rail system (aka the Tube) in London, England, with its myriad stairs and escalators, would be a real challenge for someone with reduced mobility. Many cruise ships, however, are easier to navigate thanks to their elevators and, often, a conscious focus on making the ships accessible to all.

It's a good idea to phone or e-mail the properties that you're planning to visit or the hotels that you're thinking of staying at to double-check with them that their directory information is correct and that they are indeed accessible, and to find out if they need any notice to make your visit or stay more comfortable.

There are a number of organizations and websites that offer directories of accessible sites and tips for travel. You may want to start with the Society for Accessible Travel & Hospitality (SATH) at www.sath.org.

Bringing Along Your Best Buddy: Travelling with Pets

As our pets become increasingly important parts of our lives and our families, it's only natural that we'd want to bring them along on our vacations. It will certainly limit your vacation options, but it can be a great experience for everyone, furry friends included, if you plan it right.

First, plan on driving. Bus and rail companies don't take pets (although they'll make exceptions for assistance animals such as guide dogs), and flying your pet can be a harrowing experience for both you and the animal. I strongly advise against it unless you have no other choice—for example, if you're moving. When it comes to far-away vacations, leaving your pet in the care of a trusted kennel or animal sitter is probably the more humane option. An added advantage of a sitter is that you'll have someone in the house while you're gone, which can help protect against break-ins.

If you are taking your pet, find a directory for pet-friendly hotels. Many motels and other accommodations now tolerate or even welcome pets. They generally charge an extra cleaning fee of between US$10 and US$25 per day (or, if you're lucky, per stay) and they'll often have special rules. Many don't allow you to leave a pet in your room if you're not there, for example. This is to help prevent noise and damage problems, although some may allow you to leave your pet in the room if it's in a kennel. Always check to see what the individual property's rules are. (At some Fairmont Hotels, door staff will actually take your dog for a walk if it's not a busy time of day.)

When you plan your itinerary, build in plenty of bathroom breaks for your pet, and try to keep to the same daily feeding schedule as much as possible. Always keep safety foremost in mind. Pets travelling in vehicles need to be either in kennels or in special harness-like seat belts, so that they can't interfere with the driver, and to give them some protection in case there's an accident. Be sure that your pet is tattooed or microchipped, and is wearing a collar with your cellphone number on it, just in case it gets separated from you. Always keep your dog on a leash in an unfamiliar area: you don't know the local risks, and an animal that gets spooked or is in strange surroundings may not respond to your usual commands, such as "come."

Research your planned stops ahead of time, especially if you want to tour any local attractions. Leaving your pet in your vehicle while you tour is not acceptable. On warm days, the interior of the vehicle can heat up enough to actually kill your pet. You also run the risk of having your pet stolen from your vehicle if you leave it unattended. A better option is to find a doggie daycare at your destination for the times when you want to be out touring.

Of course, it's even better if you can find fun activities to share with your pet, such as hiking. Just remember to double-check that trails and beaches are dog-friendly, for example, or allow your dog to go off-leash. Many visitors bureaus can help you find accommodation, restaurant patios, and parks that welcome pets.

PETS IN FLIGHT

If you absolutely have to fly your pet, be aware that some airlines restrict pet travel during cold and hot weather and during busy holiday periods. That's because most pets have to travel in a special area of the cargo hold, and there's a danger that it could get too cold or hot, or that the pet will be "bumped" off the flight because there's too much luggage on board. Always choose a direct flight to minimize the chances that your pet could be misdirected or delayed during a stopover.

The airlines generally require proof of vaccination, at least for rabies, and they require that the pet be in a hard-sided carrier big enough to lie down and turn around in. While it was once commonly suggested that pets be sedated, we now know that sedation can potentially be harmful because it can slow down their heart rate. Talk to your veterinarian about strategies to ease your pet's stress level when flying. The Humane Society of the United States has some excellent advice about pet travel at www.hsus.org. The bottom line is to do whatever's best for your pet. And never forget that airlines classify pets as baggage. While individual airline personnel may care very much, the airline's schedule and bottom line will always come first.

 Travel Best Bet!
In one case, a family was flying from Winnipeg to Halifax for an extended Christmas holiday, so they booked their dog on the same flights as them. They were horrified when they looked out of the window as they left their stopover in Toronto and saw the dog in its kennel sitting on the tarmac. The cargo hold had filled up, so the dog had to be flown out on a later flight. You can just imagine how the family felt until they were reunited with their beloved pet. It wasn't exactly the best start to their vacation.

Business Travel

When you're travelling for business reasons, you'll usually have a few specific priorities: staying connected to the office or your local contacts, protecting any business samples or presentations that you have with you, and making sure that your outfit for the big meeting or presentation arrives at the airport with you, for example.

As with any trip, you need to make sure that anything essential goes on the plane with you—and that includes your suit, the computer disk or USB key containing your presentation, and your cellphone or other e-mail/phone device. This can be a challenge these days with strict enforcement of carry-on luggage size and content restrictions. Check out your airline's restrictions ahead of time, and stay within them to avoid having gate personnel check your baggage into the hold at the last minute.

You could also consider using a baggage service or courier service to send samples, or even your suitcase, ahead of time. This keeps your baggage to a minimum for your journey, but you'll still have everything that you need when you get to your destination. Sending baggage ahead works best when you're not crossing international borders, because customs delays can be a wild card. If your package is stopped for inspection, which is always a possibility, it may not make it to your destination on time.

When it comes to accommodation, it can pay dividends to stay at a business-friendly hotel, one that offers high-speed modem and wireless access in the rooms, fax machines, and local free calling, or one with a decent business centre (that is, more than just a single computer sitting in the hotel lobby). If you're travelling during busy periods—especially during holidays such as Spring Break—research your hotel's location carefully. Stay away from any site that's near a beach or other area that's likely to be noisy with families or rowdy with partiers.

To keep communication expenses down, use a calling card to make or return calls. This saves you from the hotel's often exorbitant charges for long-distance calls, and can also save on cellphone roaming and long-distance charges, which also tend to be quite high.

Travel Best Bet!
One client who had a work situation come up during her vacation wasn't staying at a hotel with a business centre, and she didn't have her laptop with her. She was able to handle the work, however, because she found an Internet café with reasonable access rates nearby. She had also backed up her key files before she left, and had sent them to herself on her web-based Google e-mail address. That meant that the files were sitting in her account, giving her access to them wherever and whenever she needed them.

If you're not travelling too far, consider taking the train. It's much easier to work on board the train than on an airplane (and safer than using a cellphone or PDA while driving!), and you don't waste as much time as you would sitting in airport terminals waiting for flights. If you do fly, find out if you qualify for access to an executive-class lounge through your airline's frequent flyer program or your ticket. These can be quieter places to work than out in the main terminal, and they usually offer Internet and phone access along with greater comfort. Many airports are now incorporating "pay as you go" lounges with similar amenities. A single use might cost US$30 to US$40, which is well worth the expense if you can get a couple of hours of decent work done during a stopover.

CLAIRE'S BEST BETS FOR SPECIALTY TRAVEL

- To maximize your enjoyment of theme parks, research them thoroughly ahead of time, and have an action plan for when you arrive.

- Taking a pre-planned guided tour can save you money and planning time. Just be sure that the tour company is a good fit with your travel goals.

- Take your vacation to a whole new level by learning something new or by volunteering.

- Planning is essential for travellers with disabilities, but many attractions and accommodations are far more accessible than they used to be, which is opening up destinations around the world.

- Planning is also essential if you're travelling with pets. Do everything that you can to avoid flying with them, however, as the experience can be a source of huge stress for them (and you).

- If you're travelling on business, choose a hotel that's business-friendly and make sure that you have access to all of the electronic files that you'll need on the road.

Chapter 13
Coming Home

Duty-Free Bargains... or Not

I used to love heading to the duty-free shop in an airport on my way home from a trip. However, bargain hunters beware! I'm increasingly finding that the prices in duty-free shops aren't much better than they are at home. If you're flying out of countries that are members of the European Union you'll see that new regulations have made duty free much less of a bargain. If you're looking to save some money on a certain item, check its price before you leave home. Then you won't be stuck in a duty-free aisle wondering if the item really is good value or not.

And, of course, you'll want to know your duty-free limits in advance, too. The item you're eyeing definitely won't be a bargain if you end up paying taxes and duties on it as part of your welcome home.

A Taxing Reminder

If you have tax refund paperwork from your vacation purchases, don't forget to hand it in for processing at the airport. There will usually be signs pointing the way to the paperwork drop-off point or the kiosk where you may be able to obtain your refund on the spot. If you have any questions, feel free to ask at the airline check-in desk. Staff should be able to point you in the right direction.

The Last Red Tape: Going through Immigration and Customs

If you've been travelling internationally, part of coming home will be going through immigration and customs. You'll need to have your passport ready, and you'll likely be asked to fill out a landing card of some sort to tell customs and immigrations officials where you've been, how long you've been there, and what you're bringing back.

While you may think this is a frustrating delay in getting to where you really want to be—your own home—remember that these officials are only doing their job, and it's an important one. Although their most obvious role is checking to make sure that you're within your limits for duty- and tax-free imports on the items that you're bringing back into the country, they're also responsible for the safety of your country's borders.

For those concerned about going through immigration and customs, I always say the same thing: tell the truth, declare everything that you're bringing back home, and there won't be a problem. The problems occur when people try to lie or hide items that are either over the duty-free limit or illegal. Make sure that you have all your receipts handy and in one place in your carry-on luggage, so that they'll be easy to produce if customs officials ask for them.

Know your duty-free limits, and know what you can and can't bring back into the country. Rules vary depending on the country, but fresh food—meat, dairy products, fruits, vegetables—and nuts and seeds are usually prohibited. This is vital in order to protect the safety of the local agricultural industry, because diseases that have the potential to wipe out certain crops can be inadvertently carried on these products. That's also why you'll often be asked if you've been on a farm in the last two weeks, and whether you're planning on visiting a farm in the next two weeks. If the answer is "yes," officials may recommend certain disinfecting solutions to make sure that your footwear isn't bringing in any foreign substances. In addition, products made from endangered species are prohibited, as are antiquities and some types of weapons. There are usually limits on the amount of cash you can bring in, too.

Be prepared to prove how long you've been out of the country, especially if your government's duty-free limits increase the longer you've been away. This is straightforward if you've been flying—your tickets and your passport will show departure dates. If you've been driving or riding the rails, however, make sure that you've kept all your accommodation receipts as proof of time outside the country.

Readjusting to Life at Home

It's not unusual to feel a little let down when you come home from a lovely vacation. After all, few of us really want to return to reality: cooking our own meals, doing our own dishes, commuting to work, working!

If you can, and especially if you have a long flight or journey on your last travel day, try to build in one or two transition days at home before you have to go back to work. This gives you a chance to recover from the trip, readjust your sleep patterns, get your laundry done, and catch up on your mail and e-mail.

To ease your way back in to a regular routine—even when you're feeling a little tired or blue about that routine—try to build in some fun time or a few rewards. Maybe it's a favourite coffee or tea treat on your way to work, or wearing that great outfit you bought in a boutique you discovered near your hotel. Recognize that it's natural to wish we could work less and travel more, but recognize too that part of the fun of travel comes from it not being part of your daily routine: the novelty and the change of pace help make it special. Focus instead on what's best about being home—friends and family nearby, a comfy (bug-free!) bed to sink into at night, an entire wardrobe full of clothes (and shoes!) to choose from instead of just a suitcase, a friendly local pub or coffee shop just around the corner. Look for the positives, and I know you'll find them.

Travel Best Bet!

If you begin to feel ill within a couple of weeks of coming home from any trip, visit your doctor and let her know that you've been travelling, where you went, and what you did. It's unlikely that you picked up anything serious on your trip, but just in case you did, it's very important to catch it as quickly as possible.

Getting your photos developed and/or printed is a great way to relive your vacation. Try getting together with your travelling companions to trade photos and stories. Many people now create mini works of art with scrapbooks and photo albums. If you've fallen in love with the place you travelled to, you could even create a website all about it.

Need more inspiration? Reading great travel books can be a wonderful "escape" to warmer climes if you've come back to rain or snow. And there's absolutely nothing better than sitting down with an atlas or a pile of brochures (in paper or on the Internet) and planning your next trip. Bon voyage!

CLAIRE'S BEST BETS FOR COMING HOME

- Make sure you have all your documentation and receipts ready for inspection when you go through customs and immigration checks.

- Know your duty-free limits, and don't attempt to get away with not declaring items that are over your limit.

- Don't bring anything prohibited back with you, including fresh food, antiquities, and anything made from endangered species.

- Give yourself a break when you get home. Feeling tired or a little let down is natural, so try to ease yourself gently into your regular routine.

- Find the positives in life back home, and boost your fun factor by starting to plan your next trip!

Checklists

To-do List

AT LEAST ONE TO SIX MONTHS BEFORE YOU DEPART

- Research your destination: plan, have fun, and book your travel!
- Learn the basics of the language, if applicable.
- Check your passport, including expiry date and number of blank pages, if you're travelling to another country.
- Apply for visas for foreign countries, if applicable.
- Find out which vaccinations or medications you may need, and get them.
- Obtain notarized consent forms for children travelling with you, if applicable.
- Obtain an international driving permit, if applicable.
- Check your household, auto, and personal health insurance policies so you'll know what you need in terms of extra coverage for travel.
- Protect your travel investment with cancellation and medical insurance, at a minimum.
- Ensure that you have a written inventory of your household contents, and store it off-site.
- Make sure medical and dental exams are up to date.
- Book pets into kennels (the most popular kennels book months ahead for vacation seasons).
- Research the prices of any purchases you may want to make while on your trip.
- Check your country's duty-free limits.

AT LEAST ONE TO FOUR WEEKS BEFORE

- Keep up with the news about your destination.
- Write out your itinerary and leave it with someone you trust.
- Book reservations at tourist attractions that may be busy.
- Register expensive new items such as cameras and jewellery with the customs office, or photocopy the receipt and tuck it into your luggage.
- Obtain currency and traveller's cheques as applicable.

- Notify credit card companies of your travel plans, and check limits and expiry dates on cards.
- If you're flying, check your baggage limits and buy TSA-approved locks.
- If you're driving, take your vehicle in for a routine maintenance check.
- Tag your luggage inside and out, and add something bright around the handle.
- Check clothing in case it needs to be cleaned or repaired.

AT LEAST ONE TO SEVEN DAYS BEFORE

- Prepare your home. Test smoke detectors, check locks, ask someone you trust to handle garbage and yard chores, and set light and appliance timers.
- Cancel mail and newspaper delivery.
- Move expensive jewellery, household paperwork such as insurance policies, and small valuable items to a safety deposit box (if they're not already there).
- If you're flying, check current security regulations for carry-on luggage.
- Check the weather at your destination.
- Draw up your packing list, lay out your clothes—and pack!
- Write up your medication list and make sure you have all the prescriptions you'll need.
- Reconfirm your flights, seating, and any special meal requests 24 to 48 hours prior to flight.
- Check what (if any) food will be served on the flight, so you'll know if you need to bring any with you or set aside cash for purchasing a meal before you board or on board.
- Check with your well maintenance company to see if it's necessary to close off the water supply when you leave.
- Book taxis or shuttles to the airport as needed (taxis can often be booked 12 hours ahead of time).

DAY OF DEPARTURE

- Shut off water supply to clothes washer.
- Dispose of perishables from fridge.
- Unplug appliances and lower the thermostat and water heater settings.
- Close off your well water, if necessary.
- Unplug or switch off garage door opener.
- Remove registration and insurance information from your vehicle.
- Check the airline's website or call their toll-free number to ensure your flight is on time.
- Check in for flight online and print out your boarding pass if your airline offers this option.
- Check the traffic report in case you'll need to leave extra time to get to the airport.

Packing Lists

CARRY-ON LUGGAGE

- Allergy-safe snacks
- Camera, extra batteries, extra film or digital flash card
- Cellphone, calling card
- Change of clothes
- Items to pass the time: books, magazines, DVD player, MP3 players
- Gum or hard candy
- House and car keys
- List of emergency phone numbers, including credit card and bank notifications, and contacts back home, and for consulate or embassy, airline, vehicle rental agency
- Money (separate your cash and stash it in a couple of different places; keep travellers cheque serial numbers separate from the cheques themselves)
- Maps and guidebooks (tear out just the pages you need, to lighten your load)
- Medication (ensure name on label is exactly the same as on your passport) and medication list
- Photos of your checked luggage and a contents list (in case it gets lost)
- Sleep mask, earplugs, small blanket, or scarf
- Sunglasses (especially if you're driving)
- Sweater or jacket
- Toiletries as allowed by security regulations (toothbrush, moistened wipes, breath mints or strips at a minimum)
- Travel documents, including passport, tickets, vouchers, driver's licence, insurance, driving directions for your first destination if needed, vaccination record, doctor's letter if you're carrying syringes, medication list (consider using a neck pouch or security belt)

Travel Medical Kit

- Antibiotics (depending on where you're travelling to)
- Antihistamines or nasal decongestant spray
- Anti-itch lotion
- Antiseptic ointment
- Antiseptic towelettes
- Band-Aids
- Blister pads
- Motion sickness remedies
- Pain relievers
- Remedies for stomach upsets and diarrhea
- Small digital thermometer
- Sore throat lozenges
- Tweezers (to remove splinters)

CHECKED LUGGAGE

- Address book or address list for postcards
- Battery-operated alarm clock/radio
- Cellphone charger
- Duct tape
- Electrical converter/adapter
- Eyeglass repair kit
- Fold-away rain gear
- Inexpensive jewellery
- Luggage strap
- Mini sewing kit and lint brush
- Pen and paper

- Photocopies of key documents, such as passports
- Phrase book
- Portable smoke detector/carbon monoxide detector (check they're working before you pack them)
- Resealable plastic bags
- Rubber door stop (for hotel room doors)
- Scarf
- Small flashlight plus spare batteries
- Snacks (but no fresh food such as fruits or vegetables if you're crossing international borders)
- Spare pair of eyeglasses or extra contact lenses and solution
- Sports gear as appropriate
- Travel hairdryer (if needed)
- Travel iron or steamer (if needed)
- Umbrella
- Winter outerwear (if applicable)

Toiletries

- Cleansing and moisturizing products
- Cosmetics
- Deodorant
- Q-tips and cotton balls
- Individual sachets of bubble bath or bath salts
- Insect repellent
- Sanitary products
- Shampoo, conditioner, and styling products
- Shaver and shaving gel
- Small scissors and nail file
- Sunscreen
- Toothbrush, toothpaste, and floss
- Waterless hand cleanser

Clothes

- Dress
- Jackets
- Pants
- Shirts
- Skirts/shorts
- Sleepwear
- Socks/hose
- Sunhat
- Swimsuit and cover-up
- Ties and belts
- Underwear

Shoes

- Dress shoes
- Walking shoes
- Water/sport shoes

Kidstuff

- Books, toys, travel games, game players, CDs
- Car seat
- Kid-friendly, healthy snacks
- Portable bedrail
- Two-way radios
- Up-to-date photograph of each child, with vital statistics

And finally, don't forget to take your manners, patience, and sense of humour!

Useful Travel Websites

Accessible travel: www.sath.org

Adventure travel:
- www.adventures-abroad.com
- www.gapadventures.com

Air travel:
- www.catsa.gc.ca (for security regulations)
- www.fearofflyinghelp.com
- www.seatguru.com

Calling home: www.infocanadadirect.com

Currency conversion: www.xe.com

Duty-free allowances:
- Canada: www.cbsa-asfc.gc.ca
- United Kingdom: www.hmrc.gov.uk
- United States: www.cbp.gov

Entrance and exit requirements for different countries:
- www.voyage.gc.ca

Freighter travel:
- www.freightercruises.com
- www.freighter-travel.com

Health resources:
- Food allergy translation: www.selectwisely.com
- Foreign & Commonwealth Office (United Kingdom):
  www.fco.gov.uk
- International Association for Medical Assistance to Travellers:
  www.iamat.org
- Public Health Agency of Canada: www.phac-aspc.gc.ca
- Travel Health (United Kingdom): www.travelhealth.co.uk
- Travel Health Online: www.tripprep.com
- US Centers for Disease Control: www.cdc.gov
- US Department of State Overseas Citizens Services:
  http://travel.state.gov
- World Health Organization: www.who.int

Home exchanges: www.homeexchange.com

Hostels:
- www.hostels.com
- www.hostelworld.com
- www.hihostels.ca

Passports:
- Canada: www.voyage.gc.ca
- United Kingdom: www.ips.gov.uk
- United States: http://travel.state.gov

Pets: www.hsus.org

Research:
- www.citysearch.com
- www.hotelshark.com
- www.igougo.com
- www.lonelyplanet.com
- www.mapquest.com
- www.routestolearning.ca
- www.tripadvisor.com

Time around the world:
- www.timeanddate.com
- www.worldtimezone.com

Travel reward programs:
- www.awardplanner.com
- www.frequentflyerbonuses.com
- www.rewardscanada.ca
- www.webflyer.com

Travel advisories:
- Canada: www.voyage.gc.ca
- United Kingdom: www.fco.gov.uk
- United States: http://travel.state.gov

Travel videos:
- www.flyingmonk.com
- www.turnhere.com

Visas: www.visaconnection.com

Weather:
- www.weather.com
- www.theweathernetwork.com

Women travellers: www.journeywoman.com

Index

A

accessibility issues, 175, 188
adventure travel, 174, 188
airports
  airport codes, 97
  executive-class lounge, 179
  parking issues, 17, 43
  and rental cars, 119, 123
  security, 46, 75, 89–90
air travel
  baggage limits, 43, 46–47
  booking, 5–6, 83–89
  check-in procedures, 88–89
  child and infant restraint, 162–164
  children flying solo, 166–167
  confirming your flight, 88
  during the flight, 58–59, 93–96, 162–164
  fear of flying, 95–96
  flight delays, 87–88
  food service, 93–94
  jet lag, 56–59
  overbooked flights, 90–91
  peak-season tips, 16–18
  pets, 20, 177, 189
  and pregnancy, 64–65
  prohibited items, 89–90
  researching, 70–74, 85, 188
  rewards programs, 84, 189
  seat selection, 87, 162–164
  standby travel, 85–86
  tickets, 83, 88–89, 92
alcohol, use of, 96, 113
American Automobile Association, 133
animals
  local, 63
  pets, 20, 176–177, 189
appliances, 13–14, 40–41
ATMs, 37, 39

B

backpacks, 44
baggage. See also luggage
  insurance, 27–28
  limits, 18, 43, 46–47
bankruptcy issues, 4–5, 23–24, 73

bathrooms, finding, 159
beach vacations, 64
Bed & Breakfast inns (B&Bs), 130
bedbugs, 136–137
bereavement fares, 86
business travel, 177–178

C

calling cards, 149
calling home, 148–149
cameras, 50, 75
cancellation insurance, 25, 26–27, 70
car rental. See vehicle rental
carry-on luggage, 46, 48, 186
cellphones, 76, 80, 149
checked luggage, 46, 49–50, 186–187
Child Aviation Restraint System (CARES), 163
children. See also family travel
  documentation, 11–12, 160
  during the flight, 59, 162–164
  preparation, 157–162, 187
  and rental cars, 120, 124
  road trips, 165
  single-parent travel, 165–166
  travelling alone, 86, 166–167
citizenship, dual, 10
clothing
  for cruises, 109–110
  cultural differences, 146–147
  packing, 47, 49, 187
consumer protection, 4–5, 23–24, 73
contraband items, 152, 182
cost saving
  air fares, 84–86
  group vacations, 6–7, 172, 175
  hotels, 132–134
  off-season travel, 19, 20
  perks and upgrades, 20
  shopping, 150–152
  tax refunds, 152, 181–182
  travel traps, 70–74
country inns, 130
credit cards
  and consumer protection, 23, 73
  fraud prevention, 152

credit cards *(continued)*
    special discounts, 134
    travel rewards programs, 84
    use of, 38–39
    and vehicle insurance, 121
cruises
    cabin selection, 107
    clothing, 109–110
    cost saving, 102
    dining, 109
    disembarking, 114–115
    extra fees, 113–114
    family travel, 104–105
    gratuities, 114
    health issues, 104, 112
    motion sickness, 61, 103, 112–113
    researching, 101–102, 103–104, 112
    ship safety, 103, 108–109
    shore excursions, 110–111
    travel to, 107–108
cultural differences, 146–148
currency
    cash, 36–37, 74
    exchange, 37–38, 39, 188
    and shopping, 150
customs, 13–14, 181–182

D
debit cards, 39, 40
deep vein thrombosis (DVT), 59, 95
dehydration, 58, 61, 62
discounts. *See* cost saving
disease prevention. *See* health issues
doctors. *See* health issues
documentation
    and children, 11–12, 160
    entrance and exit, 8–9, 10, 11, 188
    landing card, 11, 181–182
    passports, 8–10, 74, 153–154, 160, 189
    picture ID, 8, 89
    spelling of name, 8, 83
    theft prevention, 74
    tourist card, 11
    use of maiden name, 171
    visas, 11, 189
duty-free allowances, 13–14, 181–182, 188

E
ears and sinuses, 58–59, 163
electrical appliances, 13–14, 40–41
electrical supply, 40–41
entrance and exit requirements, 8–9, 10, 11, 188
etiquette, 143–144, 146–148
export/import regulations, 152, 182
eyeglasses, 58, 63

F
family travel. *See also* children
    cruises, 104–105
    preparation, 157–162
    single-parent travel, 165–166
    theme parks, 169–170
fear of flying, 95–96
food allergies, 58, 60, 112
food poisoning, 60–61
food products, restricted, 152, 182
foreign languages, 14–16, 60, 189
fraud prevention
    credit cards, 152
    electronic key cards, 139
    travel deals, 73–74
freighter travel, 102, 188

G
gifts, transport of, 17, 43
gratuities, 114, 138, 144–146
group vacations, 6–7, 172, 175
guided tours, 172–174

H
health issues
    after returning home, 66, 182–183
    dehydration, 58, 61
    disease prevention, 53–55, 159
    drinking water, 59–60, 62, 112
    during the flight, 58–59, 163
    food poisoning, 60–61
    hygiene habits, 60, 63
    illness, 61–64, 112
    insects, 63, 136–137
    jet lag, 56–59
    medical assistance, 61, 62–63
    medication, 54–55, 56, 161
    motion sickness, 61, 103, 112–113, 165

researching, 55, 62, 188
home exchange, 131–132, 189
home security, 41–43
honeymoon vacations, 170–172
hostels, 129, 189
hotels
    billing issues, 139
    complaint procedures, 136, 140
    extra fees, 137–138
    insect infestations, 136–137
    and language help, 15–16
    parking issues, 77
    pets, 176
    researching, 130, 132–134, 189
    room reservations, 134–135, 139
    room service, 138
    security, 79–80
    telephones, 149, 178

I
identification
    and full name, 8, 83, 89
    passports, 8–10, 74, 153–154, 160, 189
    picture ID, 8, 89
    tags for luggage, 18, 44, 45
    use of maiden name, 171
illegal products, 152, 182
illness. See also health issues
    after returning home, 66, 182–183
    and travel, 61–64, 112
insects, 63, 136–137
insurance
    baggage, 27–28
    cancellation, 25, 26–27, 70
    cost saving, 25
    importance of, 23–24
    making a claim, 26, 31–32
    medical, 24–26, 28–30, 54, 62
    providers, 24–26, 31
    and travel advisories, 30–31
    vehicle rental, 121–122, 126
International Certificate of Vaccination, 54
international driving permits, 12–13, 122
Internet use
    banking, 39
    booking online, 5–6, 73–74, 88–89
    e-mail, 7, 148–149

finding bathrooms, 159
useful websites, 188–189
vacation destinations, 2, 131
itinerary
    and children, 157–159
    flexibility, 143–144, 153
    planning, 35–36, 57
    returning home, 182–183

J
jet lag, 56–59
jewellery, 13–14, 150

L
landing card, 11, 181–182
language issues, 14–16, 60
learning adventures, 173
lice, 136–137
luggage. See also packing
    airport security, 46, 75, 89–90
    carry-on bags, 46, 48
    checked bags, 46, 49–50, 186–187
    identifying, 18, 44, 45
    insurance, 27–28
    limits, 18, 43, 46–47
    locks, 44–45, 75
    loss or damage, 27–28, 45, 96–99
    options, 43–45
    packing, 45–50
    theft prevention, 74–75

M
malaria, 54, 63
maps, road, 124–125
marriage, destination weddings, 172
medical insurance, 24–26, 28–30, 54, 62
medical kit, 54, 159, 186
medication, 54–55, 56, 161
men's vacations, 175
money. See currency
mosquitoes, 63
motels, 129
motion sickness, 61, 103, 112–113, 165

N
norovirus (Norwalk-like virus), 112

O
off-season travel, 19, 20, 169

P
packing. *See also* luggage
    checklist, 186–187
    and children, 161
    documentation, 36
    emergency kit, 80
    new-looking items, 13–14
    tips, 45–50
panhandlers, 147–148
passports
    dual citizenship, 10
    entering US, 8
    loss of, 153–154
    obtaining, 9–10, 160, 189
    theft prevention, 74
PayPal, 74
peak season travel tips, 16–19
pets, 20, 176–177, 189
photography restrictions, 70
phrase books, 15–16
pick pocket prevention, 74, 77–78, 147–148
planning. *See* vacation planning
points systems, 84–85
politically unstable areas, 80
pregnancy, 64–65
prohibited items
    and air travel, 89–90
    illegal products, 152, 182

R
rental properties, 131
research. *See* vacation planning
resorts, 130–131, 166
rewards programs, 84–85, 189

S
safety, 74–81
seasickness. *See* motion sickness
seniors, vehicle rental, 121
shopping
    aggressive salespeople, 147–148
    baggage limits, 46
    bargaining tips, 150–152
    on cruises, 111
    duty-free, 13–14, 181–182, 188
    illegal products, 152, 182
    tax refunds, 152, 181–182
    in the United States, 152
sightseeing
    cultural differences, 146–148
    finding bathrooms, 159
    reservations for, 16–17, 18
    shore excursions, 110–111
sleep, tips, 56–57, 135–136
summer travel, 20
swimming, 64

T
taxi cabs, 15–16, 77, 144
tax refunds, 152, 181–182
telephones
    cellphones, 76, 80, 149
    cost saving, 149, 178, 188
theft prevention, 74–75, 77–78, 113, 147–148
theme parks, 169–170
tickets, airline, 83, 88–89, 92
timeshare properties, 72
time zones, 14, 189
tipping, 114, 138, 144–146
toiletries, 47–48, 187
tourist or landing cards, 11
translators, pocket, 15
travel advisories
    and insurance, 30–31
    political instability, 80
    use of, 69–70
    websites, 5, 69, 189
travel agents or advisers
    discounts for, 73
    group vacations, 7
    selecting, 3–5
    specialty travel, 4, 115
    travel service industry, 70–74
travel clubs, 72
travel insurance. *See* insurance
traveller's cheques and cheque cards, 39–40, 74
travel videos, 2, 189

V
vacation planning
    checklists, 184–187

and children, 157–159
choices, 1–2
flexibility, 143–144, 153
home security, 41–43
itinerary planning, 35–36, 57
off-season travel, 19, 20, 169
peak travel periods, 16–19
and pets, 176–177, 189
researching, 2, 5–6, 131, 188–189
returning home, 182–183
travel traps, 70–74
useful websites, 188–189
vacation properties, 72
vaccinations, 53, 54–55
vehicle rental
accidents and breakdowns, 125–126
extra fees, 119–121
insurance, 121–122, 126
international driving permits, 12–13, 122
left-hand-drive countries, 127
pickup and return, 122–124, 126
reservations, 117–119
road safety, 64, 124–125
and spare eyeglasses, 63
visas, 11, 189
volunteer vacations, 174

W
water, drinking, 59–60, 62, 112
weather
off-season travel, 19, 20
reports, 19, 189
researching risks, 70
travel delays, 17
websites. *See also* Internet use
list of, 188–189
weddings, 172
winter travel, 19–20
women's issues
cultural differences, 147
girls' getaways, 175
pregnancy, 64–65
travelling alone, 78–79, 189